MW00325184

Philosophical Foundations of the Cognitive Science of Religion

A Head Start

Robert N. McCauley

with

E. Thomas Lawson

BLOOMSBURY ACADEMIC

LONDON · NEW YORK · OXFORD · NEW DELHI · SYDNEY

BLOOMSBURY ACADEMIC
Bloomsbury Publishing Plc
50 Bedford Square, London, WC1B 3DP, UK
1385 Broadway, New York, NY 10018, USA

BLOOMSBURY, BLOOMSBURY ACADEMIC and the Diana logo
are trademarks of Bloomsbury Publishing Plc

First published 2017
Paperback edition first published 2019

A catalogue record for this book is available from the British Library.

Library of Congress Cataloging-in-Publication Data
Names: McCauley, Robert N., author.
Title: Philosophical foundations of the cognitive science of religion :
a head start / Robert N. McCauley, with E. Thomas Lawson.
Description: New York : Bloomsbury Academic, 2017. |
Series: Scientific studies of religion: inquiry and explanation |
Includes bibliographical references and index.
Identifiers: LCCN 2017008509| ISBN 9781350030312 (hb) |
ISBN 9781350030336 (epub)
Subjects: LCSH: Religion. | Cognitive psychology. | Religion and culture.
Classification: LCC BL53 .M28 2017 | DDC 200.1/9–dc23
LC record available at https://lccn.loc.gov/2017008509

ISBN: HB: 978-1-3500-3031-2
      PB: 978-1-3501-0586-7
      ePDF: 978-1-3500-3032-9
      ePub: 978-1-3500-3033-6

Typeset by Integra Software Services Pvt. Ltd.

To find out more about our authors and books visit
www.bloomsbury.com and sign up for our newsletters.

Contents

List of Figures

Preface

Initiating the cognitive science of religion (CSR) required as much philosophizing as it did theorizing. Surprisingly, after more than twenty years of progress, sustaining CSR in the face of unfriendly reactions has continued to call for further philosophical defense. I have assembled this collection of philosophical essays (three of which I wrote in collaboration with Tom Lawson) and written a new chapter (6), in response to multiple requests from colleagues, including Luther Martin and Don Wiebe, the editors of this series. I had three principal aims: first, to consolidate some of that foundational philosophical work and make it more readily available; second, to highlight (in Chapter 6) new philosophical considerations that have arisen in light of that more-than-two-decades of progress in the field; and, third, where the analyses are sound, to help both practitioners and philosophical friends of CSR avoid reinventing the wheel.

Although when they first appeared some of the chapters in this book made plenty of heads start, the aim in assembling them here is to provide a head start to those interested in these matters. I trust that at the very least both friends and foes of CSR will find the arguments herein engaging and provocative. I hope that they will also find them persuasive and fruitful.

With only some minor editing to standardize the text, to correct a few errors in the originals, and to eliminate extraneous internal references (in Chapter 2), the previously published papers collected herein appear, basically, as they did when they were first published. In those papers for which Tom Lawson was my co-author, I have retained plural pronouns, when they arose, and I have kept references to the original papers in the internal references in this book (as noted in the book's reference list).

Acknowledgments

I am grateful to the publishers—Routledge, Brill, Cambridge University Press, and Oxford University Press—and to E. Thomas Lawson for permission to reprint the various papers following:

McCauley, R. N. (2014). "Explanatory Pluralism and the Cognitive Science of Religion: Or Why Scholars in Religious Studies Should Stop Worrying about Reductionism," *Mental Culture: Classical Social Theory and the Cognitive Science of Religion*. D. Xygalatas and W. W. McCorkle, Jr. (eds). London: Routledge, pp. 11–32.

Lawson, E. T. and McCauley, R. N. (1990). "Interpretation and Explanation: Problems and Promise in the Study of Religion," *Rethinking Religion: Connecting Cognition and Culture*. Cambridge: Cambridge University Press, pp. 12–31.

Lawson, E. T. and McCauley, R. N. (1993). "Crisis of Conscience, Riddle of Identity: Making Space for a Cognitive Approach to Religious Phenomena," *Journal of the American Academy of Religion*, 61: 201–223.

McCauley, R. N. and Lawson, E. T. (1996). "Who Owns 'Culture'?" *Method and Theory in the Study of Religion*, 8: 171–190.

McCauley, R. N. (2000). "Overcoming Barriers to a Cognitive Psychology of Religion," in A. Geertz and R. McCutcheon (eds.), *Perspectives on Method and Theory in the Study of Religion*, 141–161, The Hague: Brill.

Each is reprinted by permission from the respective publishers.

Numerous people have aided me in the production of this book, including Charlotte Blank, Katie Duval, Julia Marshall, William Rohde, and Whitney Taylor. I am particularly grateful to Mathew Homan for his aid and to Shiela Shinholster for the production of the diagrams in Chapter 1. I wish to thank them all.

Tom Lawson combines all of the virtues of an accomplished artist, a dedicated teacher, and a hardworking philosopher, who also happens to be incurably optimistic and cheerful. All of this makes him both a wondrous human being and the perfect collaborator. Tom and I have known one another for forty-three years. He was my teacher for two years, my mentor for a decade or so, and the friend of a lifetime. We began working together in 1980 (on the first version of what was to become the fifth chapter of *Rethinking Religion*) and published our first collaborative paper in 1984. We have published collaborative work as recently as 2007. Over that twenty-three year span we collaborated on two books and eight papers. Three of those collaborative works appear in this book. I am grateful to Tom for his permission to publish them here. My debts to Tom are many and my gratitude to him is endless.

I also wish to thank the editors of this series, Luther Martin and Don Wiebe, who have encouraged and supported the production of this book at every step. They proposed that I produce such a book a decade ago (before this series even existed!). They have exhibited admirable patience as I became, shortly after they approached me about this project, the inaugural Director of the Center for Mind, Brain, and Culture at Emory University—a position that I held for more than eight years. Starting a new Center and writing books at the same time is a challenge, and one book that required completion was in line ahead of this one. As the time passed Luther and Don prodded and nudged, but they never hedged nor stepped back. They never blinked. They never stopped believing in the importance of this project, and I am deeply grateful to them both.

Luther and Don are also among those at the top of the list of people who have influenced my thinking for the better with regard to the issues addressed in this book. Reflecting on all of the people with whom I have discussed these ideas since the mid-1980s, when Tom Lawson and I undertook the earliest of the pieces in this volume (Chapter 2), I see that that list would easily number in triple digits. After that much time, with a memory no better than mine, the risk of omitting at least a dozen or two is acute, so I will forego any attempt to name them. Suffice it to say, first, that I am profoundly grateful to scores of colleagues and friends for the seriousness with which they have taken my projects and positions, and, second, that the errors and problems that remain in this book are my responsibility.

For reasons outlined in the opening paragraphs of the first chapter of this book, I have spent the entirety of my career interacting with scholars from multiple disciplines, in addition to those from religious studies. Those disciplines include most of the core contributors to cognitive science, viz., psychology, linguistics, anthropology, neuroscience, and philosophy. I spent what I regarded as five idyllic years in graduate school at the University of Chicago—the final four devoted to earning my Ph.D. in the philosophy of science. It is fair to say that on the whole philosophers both were and have remained a good deal more receptive to my ideas about the cognitive science of religion than is true of scholars of religion.

During those four years in the Department of Philosophy at Chicago, I made a half dozen friendships that thrive to this day. Among those friends, Mark Johnson and Bill Bechtel have remained particularly helpful and sympathetic auditors of my work—both in philosophy and in the cognitive science of religion. I am profoundly grateful to both, whose work I admire unequivocally and from which I have learned so much. I am thankful not just for decades of intellectual engagement, stimulation, and support but for Mark and Sandra McMorris Johnson and Bill Bechtel and Adele Abrahamsen's *thousands* of kindnesses to me and to my family over those years as well.

Within a year of completing graduate school, I met Paul Thagard, who, I realized in fairly short order, possessed an outstanding mind, combined with a huge measure of wit, warmth, and decency. Like Mark and Bill, Paul was another incredibly able, productive, and personable colleague, who was interested and sympathetic from the start not only with my views in the philosophy of science about cross-scientific relations but with my arguments for the power of the methods, theories, and findings of the cognitive sciences to illuminate religious thought and conduct. I have benefitted immeasurably— again, as with Mark and Bill—for more than thirty years now from engaging with Paul's own work and from his aid and encouragement of mine.

It is a pleasure to state publically the joy and gratitude I feel about the fact that I have had the friendship and support of three of the finest minds of my generation, and it is to them—Mark, Bill, and Paul—that I dedicate this book.

In one crucial direction, of course, my joy and gratitude extend even further. I wish to thank my wife, Dorinda McCauley, for her unfailing support of my intellectual work and of my efforts on this book, in particular. I am grateful for her scores of perceptive editorial comments and stylistic suggestions. With these as with so much else in our life together, she has been a loving and thoughtful partner.

Robert N. McCauley
Center for Mind, Brain, and Culture
Emory University
Atlanta, Georgia, USA

Explanatory Pluralism and the Cognitive Science of Religion: Or Why Scholars in Religious Studies Should Stop Worrying about Reductionism

Prologue

Nearly forty years ago when I was a graduate student (at the Divinity School of the University of Chicago) trying to envision how the theoretical tools, the findings, and the methods of the cognitive sciences might be brought to bear on religious phenomena, the *universal* response that such speculations elicited was some variation or other on the comment "Oh!… you are a *reductionist*." The comment, uttered with the hint of a sneer, suggested something akin to either disgust or contempt.

Unfortunately, but not surprisingly, it took *leaving* the field of religious studies for me to find more hospitable intellectual environs in which to pursue and develop those ideas. I have spent most of my subsequent career among philosophers and practitioners of the psychological, cognitive, and neuro-sciences. In the 1990s, after Tom Lawson and I (both jointly and individually) had begun to publish our ideas about carrying out a cognitive science of religion, I began, once again, to travel in the world of religious studies.

Lawson and I argued for the interdependence of explanatory and interpretive enterprises in inquires about human affairs and expressed our concern, simply, to redress what seemed to us to be a serious imbalance in religious studies in favor of the latter (Lawson and McCauley 1990: 13 and 22–31). In the twenty-plus years since, wariness about our and others' explanatory proposals persists in many quarters (examples include Buckley and Buckley 1995; Bell 2005; however, see Lawson and McCauley 1995). Fortunately, in the meantime, others have argued for the same sort of *productive* engagement for which we argued between work in religious studies and explanatory projects in the cognitive science of religion (see Tite 2004; Slingerland 2008; Saler 2009).

This chapter is a further attempt to reassure those who are concerned with the religious, the meaningful, the spiritual, the subjective, the conscious, the experiential, the historical, the sociocultural, and the culturally constructed (and with the details of each), that neither the substantial growth of the cognitive science of religion over the past two decades, nor its ongoing progress, poses any threat to their concerns or to their objects of study. The reasons for that are legion; however, here I intend to focus on but one consideration concerning the character of what has traditionally been referred to as "reduction" in science. Specifically, religion scholars' worries about cognitive science explaining away the religious, the meaningful, the spiritual, and so on presume a coarse-grained and unsatisfactory model of cross-scientific relations that has undergone withering criticism in the philosophy of science.

After a preliminary comment criticizing loose talk about reduction in popular discourse, in religious studies, in the humanities, and even in some of the social sciences, I shall offer a brief overview of levels of analysis in science and of the models of reduction in science of the logical empiricists and of the New Wave reductionists. Then I will differentiate two different kinds of reductive relations that arise between scientific projects. I will argue that the major worries of scholars of religion about the powers of cognitive theories of religion to eliminate the religious, the meaningful, the spiritual, and so on confuse these two sorts of reductive contexts. The explanatory pluralist model of cross-scientific relations illuminates the kind of multidisciplinary programs of research that are pursued both in the contemporary cognitive sciences generally and in the cognitive science of religion.

In a brief final section, I will illustrate the explanatory pluralist's contention that the cognitive science of religion inevitably looks to conventional religious studies for help and guidance, and, thus, show why (a) scientism, (b) methodological exclusivism, and (c) worries about eliminativism are so wrong-headed. Explanatory pluralism stresses, first, that science is not the only game in town and that it is not the only way that we acquire knowledge (no scientism). Consequently, second, if they ignore one another, traditional religious studies and the cognitive science of religion will each be done less well than they can be (no methodological exclusivism). And, third, the cognitive science of religion will not eliminate the religious, the meaningful, the spiritual, and so on (no eliminativism). For the sake of brevity, I will focus in the discussion that follows on the religious, since all of the others (the meaningful, the spiritual, the subjective, etc.) have served as the bases for arguments for the uniqueness or the autonomy or the specialness of the religious at one time or another.

What the cognitive science of religion may do on such fronts, if anything, is *vindicate* the key contributions that scholars studying such matters can make to our understanding of the phenomena at issue. What it certainly has done and will continue to do is enrich our understanding of those phenomena by showing how they connect with operations of the human mind/brain, which is both embodied and embedded in traditions, cultures, and discourses. The cognitive science of religion does so by enlisting and integrating both the findings and the methods of at least a half dozen different scientific approaches and their concomitant theoretical perspectives. Those perspectives include the cognitive, developmental, comparative, evolutionary, neural, and archaeological, to name but some of the most prominent. Cognitive scientists of religion have begun to deploy those methods to generate all sorts of new evidence bearing on our understanding of both religious systems and individuals' religious cognition and conduct.

A preliminary

Science is opportunistic. Scientists will consider evidence wherever they find it, and anything that we know about the world may prove relevant to their assessments of any particular scientific hypothesis. Finally, this should be true for any hypothesis (scientific or not), and, just as finally, such attention to bona fide evidence is the mark of the reasonableness of *any* inquiry, not just scientific inquiries. (The salient difference between the sciences and other inquiries concerns their focus on discovering, discerning, collecting, recording, generating, analyzing, and assessing *empirical* evidence.)

Special pleading arises when inquirers in some field abandon such evidential opportunism (Fodor 1983: 106). They seek to insulate cherished commitments from some of, or the entire, evidential onslaught. Various disciplines, including sciences, have had periods when some or even most of their practitioners resorted to special pleading. Examples include protecting vitalism in the biological sciences in the late nineteenth and early twentieth centuries and insisting in the social sciences on the primacy of social facts or thick descriptions (Durkheim 1964; Geertz 1973).

Religions famously do their special pleading upfront, so, perhaps, it should come as no surprise that religious studies has been plagued, throughout its history, with a penchant for special pleading too. In its scholarly guise, special pleading in religious studies has taken a variety of forms, beyond those it borrows from the social sciences. These have included claims that religious phenomena are, in all interesting respects, *sui generis* or that inquiries about religion *must* be autonomous or antireductionist. Assertions about the need for special methods to study religious phenomena have typically accompanied such claims.

Compared to the blanket antireductionism that scholars of previous generations affirmed, more recently special pleading in religious studies has adopted forms that do not appear merely to be benign but to be both true and reasonable as well. These days it turns out that each and every *particular* scientific explanation of religious phenomena just happens to be reductionist and, thus, unacceptable. In each case, the evidence for that charge is that these explanations are insufficient or incomplete. Reductionist explanations, after all, *reduce!* They always remove or ignore something; otherwise, they would not count as reductions. Consequently, critics fault them for failing to supply *full* explanations and, thus, deem them unsatisfactory and even unacceptable. The charges are true, but the conclusions are neither reasonable nor benign.

Whether it employs the older, blanket strategy or the contemporary one of disqualifying each and every explanatory proposal on a case-by-case basis, antireductionist special pleading holds, in effect, that *all* scientific explanations are, ultimately, reductionist by virtue of the fact that they all pick and choose among phenomena. Science employs theories and theories are invariably selective.

Note, however, that to be antireductionist in this sweeping sense is to be anti-explanatory, antiscientific, and antitheoretical. It is hyper-antireductionism. For the adjective "reductive" to carry any import when modifying the term "explanation," it must pick out some subset of explanations that are objectionable. If the presumption is that *all* explanations are reductive, then opposing reductive explanation is just to oppose explanatory approaches across the board. In light of the modern sciences' successes with regard to explanation, prediction, and control over the past 400 years, such hyper-antireductionism is unreasonable and obscurantist. Arguably, no heuristic of discovery in modern science has been any more productive and successful than reductionism.

The standard rejoinder at this point is to reply that the objectionable subset of reductionist explanations is the subset of those that concern some or all of the religious, the meaningful, the spiritual, and so on. The inevitable selectivity of explanatory theories in these domains, critics avow, disregards or discards something that matters (about us!). Two comments must suffice.

First, hyper-antireductionist thinkers are correct that complete, full, sufficient, or (fully) adequate explanations in science do not exist. (Ironically, it is only in religion that such explanatory presumptions arise!) But the bad news is that to say, therefore, that an explanation fails to meet such standards, that is, that it is not complete or full or sufficient or fully adequate, is no interesting criticism at all. No scientific explanations meet such standards. In science, all explanations are partial. There is no such thing as an exhaustive scientific explanation.

Second, what *matters* is always a function of the interests and problems of the inquirer. What we are inclined to take as criteria for explanatory sufficiency or adequacy are always relative to our interests and the problems that inform them. Basically, the complaints of hyper-antireductionists in religious studies amount to pointing out that their interests differ from those who are interested in explanation. Certainly, these antireductionists need not apologize for their interests; however, *nothing* follows about the un-satisfactoriness or the unacceptability of explanatory proposals *qua* explanatory proposals, and to the extent that antireductionists' special pleading forestalls not only the checks and balances but, as I shall argue, the opportunities that will arise from integration with other related inquiries, their grumblings fail to advance our knowledge.

Levels of analysis in science

Less immoderate talk about scientific reduction reliably depends on common assumptions about levels of analysis in science and their hierarchical arrangement. Such talk typically looks to the relations of parts and wholes (i.e., "mereological" relations) in nature and, specifically, to their implications for things' relative sizes. A consequence of using considerations of scale for differentiating levels in nature and levels of analysis in science is that higher level sciences treat big things and the lower level sciences treat progressively smaller things. The physical sciences are the most fundamental sciences and operate at the lowest levels of analysis, because they deal with the smallest things that are the parts of everything else. The biological sciences treat larger systems that involve more complex physical arrangements. The psychological and social sciences tackle larger systems still. At least some of the time, psychology examines organisms situated in physical and social environments, and the sociocultural sciences address large collections of psychological systems that are causally connected in sociocultural networks.

Even when looking at the broad families of sciences, an account of organizational levels in nature and of analytical levels in science that appeals to considerations of scale will prove inadequate. Not all big things with many parts (e.g., asteroids and sand dunes) are highly integrated systems that demand higher level analyses. The physical sciences not only address subatomic particles but avalanches, weather systems, and stars. The biological sciences investigate not only molecular genetics but the evolution of populations. The standard conception of analytical levels in terms of the size of the things they discuss fails to situate sciences like meteorology, geology, astrophysics, ecology, and evolutionary biology.

Organizational and contextual considerations inspire mechanists' accounts of analytical levels. Mechanists argue that attention to the organization and operations of situated mechanisms and to the local view of analytical levels that results eviscerates presumptions about lower levels' causal closure and the putative comprehensiveness of lower level explanations (Bechtel 2006, 2007: 182; Craver 2007; Craver and Bechtel 2007). Mechanists are agnostic about the generalizability of the resulting pictures of analytical levels and have abandoned characterizations of the sciences' connections overall. With their reservations in mind, the question of salvaging any plausible global account of analytical levels looms. Still, whether in scholarly debates or more popular disputations, many controversies that modern science inspires, including those swirling around reduction, presume that a general account of analytical levels is available. The mechanists are unquestionably right that in each case the details matter, but that need not rule out the search for ways to talk more carefully either about those larger issues or the arrangement of the sciences they presume (see Rosenberg 2006: 40).

Three considerations can help with the latter task. These three are independent of one another and each point to roughly similar arrangements among the major families of sciences, at least.

The first looks to a science's comparative explanatory *scope*. The lower an analytical level the wider is the corresponding science's scope. All of the phenomena studied at higher levels are describable at lower levels, but the opposite is not true. Subatomic particles are the building blocks of all other physical systems (from atoms to galaxies and from DNA to societies). The range of things a higher level concentrates on constitutes a subset of those dealt with by lower level sciences. This criterion delineates a salient respect in which lower level sciences *are* more fundamental, since they possess resources for describing a wider range of phenomena.

The order of analytical levels also corresponds to the chronological *order in natural history* that various systems evolved. The lower a science's analytical level, the longer the things to which it primarily attends have existed. For example, the subatomic particles and atoms that are the principal objects of study in the basic physical sciences appeared quite soon after the Big Bang whereas the systems that the biological sciences scrutinize first began to appear (on Earth, at least) but a few billion years ago. Developed nervous systems, brains, and the minds that eventually seemed to have accompanied them, by contrast, look to be at least a couple of billion years newer. And, finally, cultural systems that the sociocultural sciences investigate date from a few million years ago on the most optimistic estimates and, perhaps, no more than some tens of thousands of years ago on more demanding criteria.

A third consideration, the *complexity of phenomena*, is intuitively compelling, even if it defies precise description. The intuition is that each higher level deals with progressively more complex phenomena. Mind/brains seem more complex than cells, which, in turn, seem more complex than molecules. Mereological considerations may point in this direction, but by themselves, they are, again, inadequate. Our sense of a system's complexity, regardless of its size, depends on whether or not wholes are notably organized or are simply aggregates of their parts (Wimsatt 1986, 1997, 2007: Chapter 9). With neither settled criteria of complexity nor a general measure of systems' comparative integration, this consideration remains only a rough intuition for now. It is unclear how much weight it can bear in the discrimination of analytical levels in science, but scholars are bringing sophisticated, new computational tools and models to the treatment of these questions (Mitchell 2009). Figure 1.1 summarizes how these criteria organize the analytical levels of science.

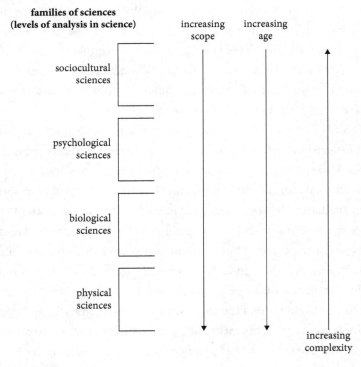

Figure 1.1 Families of sciences.

Traditional reductionism and New Wave reductionism

Some philosophical models of reduction in science would substantiate the fears of scholars in religious studies about the cognitive science of religion, since those models suggest that the cognitive scientists' explanatory proposals might explain the religious, the meaningful, the spiritual, and so on *away*. New Wave reductionists (Hooker 1981; P. M. Churchland and P. S. Churchland 1990; Bickle 1998, 2003) offer an *all-purpose*, one-size-fits-all model of reduction. Like the logical empiricists before them, they presume that accounts of the structural relations of scientific theories' explanatory principles (e.g., laws) and of the things that those theories describe exhaust what is of ontological and epistemological interest in such comparisons. Elsewhere I have argued that New Wave proposals downplay epistemologically significant features of the relevant sorts of scientific research (McCauley 1996, 2007). I have also argued that the New Wave models fail to discriminate between two crucially different classes of intertheoretic relations (McCauley 1986a, 1996, 2007). It is this second flaw on which I shall elaborate here, for it motivates the New Wavers' overly broad conclusions about elimination in science that seems to justify the antireductionists' fears about the cognitive science of religion.

On the standard logical empiricist model (Nagel 1961), scientific reduction involves deducing the laws of one scientific theory (the reduced theory, for example, the laws of classical thermodynamics) from those of another (the reducing theory, for example, the principles of statistical mechanics). This inference requires supplementing the laws of the reducing theory with a set of statements (variously known as "bridge principles," "coordinating definitions," and "reduction functions") that lay out systematic logical and material connections between the two theories' predicates, while incorporating the boundary conditions within which those connections are realized.

The standard view construes reductions as a type of explanation in which the item getting explained (the *explanandum*) is *not* some phenomenon but rather some law or other of the reduced theory. A successful reduction demonstrates how the reducing theory's explanatory resources encompass those of the reduced theory. Thus, in effect, the reduced theory constitutes an application of the reducing theory in one of its sub-domains specified by the boundary conditions.

The bridge principles must ensure the "derivability" of the reduced theory from the reducing theory by articulating connections between the two theories' predicates of sufficient logical strength to support the derivation. The bridge principles should also justify a metaphysical unity in science. They have to certify substantial links between the entities and their properties that the two theories discuss, that is, to certify their "connectability" (Nagel 1961). Establishing such connections between scientific theories motivates *programs* for unifying science via "microreductions" (Oppenheim and Putnam 1958; Causey 1977). These programs fashion a case based on mereological relations for a materialist metaphysics and envisions the reduction of entire sciences. They foresee the possibility of scientists eventually abandoning research at higher levels in deference to explanations at lower levels (P. M. Churchland 1979; P. S. Churchland 1986; Bickle 1998, 2003). Proposals differ about the logical and material strength of the bridge principles; however, all foresee a comprehensive mapping of the reduced theory's ontology on to that of the reducing theory (Nagel 1961: 354–355; Causey 1977).

The appeal of the standard model's formality, clarity, and precision is uncontested. Philosophers, however, began to realize that its idealized account of intertheoretic relations came at the price of its ability to capture many cases of intertheoretic relations that did not meet its exacting standards (Wimsatt 1978). The resulting connections frequently seemed capable of sustaining neither the derivation of the reduced theory nor the comprehensive mapping of its ontology on to the reducing theory's ontology. (Contrast, for example, Patricia Churchland's diverging assessments of the prospects for the reduction of various aspects of consciousness: P. S. Churchland 1983, 1986; P. M. Churchland and P. S. Churchland 1996.)

This diagnosis is consonant with the impression that the reducing theory's resources often do not merely encompass those of the reduced theory. On the basis of its added precision alone, the reducing theory usually appears to *improve* upon the reduced theory's account of things. For example, the articulated picture of the numerous connections permitting the sharing of information in the processing streams of the "what" and "where" pathways of primate visual systems, as presented by van Essen and Gallant (1994), arguably constitutes a correction of the initial proposal of Ungerleider and Mishkin, which construed these subsystems' operations as basically independent (Ungerleider and Mishkin 1982; Mishkin et al. 1983).

On the standard model of reduction, though, if reducing theories *correct* reduced theories, then the reduced theories' laws should *not* follow deductively from premises about the reducing theory's laws and the bridge principles. With some of history's most impressive reductions, the logical empiricists faced the embarrassing dilemma of either repudiating their deductive model of explanation or accepting bridge principles that leave enough semantic slack to render the putative derivation guilty of equivocation (Wimsatt 1976: 218; P. M. Churchland 1989: 48).

New Wave reductionists regard our *inability* to sustain bridge principles capable of underwriting the derivation of the reduced theory's regularities as a *virtue* of any putative reduction that improves upon those regularities. Instead of standing by a formally perspicuous, idealized model of reduction that fails to describe many cases, the New Wavers hold that the reducing theory explains only an *analogue* of the reduced theory constructed within the reducing theory's conceptual framework. This enables the reducing theory simultaneously to correct the reduced theory and to explain at least something very much like it. Moreover, relying on analogy, the New Wave model of reduction, apparently, accomplishes all of this without needing to specify bridge principles (however, see Endicott 1998: 71–72). The strength of the analogy can vary considerably from one case to another, resulting in a spectrum of analogical strength that ranges from retentive reduction at one end to outright theory replacement at the other. See Figure 1.2.

Although analogies fail to meet the constraints of the standard model, they do undergird a picture of *approximate reduction* that embraces the familiar cases. On the New Wave account, the standard model's ideal designates an end point on the continuum of the comparative levels of isomorphism between reduced theories and their analogues. If even the standard model's parade cases from the physical sciences, in fact, fall short of the anchor point that designates

Figure 1.2 New Wave continuum model.

that ideal on this continuum, then that would only underscore the significance of New Wave analyses' abilities to make sense of these many familiar cases of approximate reduction. On the New Wave account, the standard model's parade cases *are* only approximate reductions, since they reliably require counterfactual assumptions (Bickle 1998: 38, 2003: 11).

Distinguishing cross-scientific and successor contexts

The New Wavers' continuum orders the relative goodness-of-mapping relations possible between reduced theories and their images constructed within the frameworks of their corresponding reducing theories. None of the New Wave reductionists, though, offer any precise criteria for when the slack becomes intolerable, that is, when the theory-analogue's approximation of the reduced theory becomes too loose to make sense of reductive talk (Bickle 1998: 100–101). At some point on that continuum the goodness-of-mapping becomes sufficiently weak that the case for intertheoretic continuity collapses.

According to New Wavers such situations do not yield reductions but, instead, the "historical theory succession" that marks scientific revolutions (Bickle 1998: 101). New Wave reductionists take inspiration from Paul Feyerabend and Thomas Kuhn's objections to the logical empiricists' standard model (Feyerabend 1962; Kuhn 1970). In scientific revolutions the superior theory simply displaces its inferior predecessor. If their intertheoretic mappings are as tenuous as those in uncontroversial historical cases such as between Stahl's account of combustion and Lavoisier's or between Gall's phrenological hypotheses and modern cognitive neuroscience, we are, presumably, justified in speaking of the complete *elimination* of the inferior theory.

As grounds for constructing an analogue of the reduced theory dwindle, cases are arrayed further and further to the right on the continuum in Figure 1.2. On the New Wave account the prospects for retaining either the principles or the ontology of the theory to be reduced decrease as cases exhibit fewer and fewer correspondences. In the right half of the continuum, the outlook for reconciling the two theories moves from dim to dismal. New Wave reductionists maintain that the failure of intertheoretic mapping in the dismal cases is so thoroughgoing that the success of the reducing theory impugns the integrity of the reduced theory and motivates its outright rejection. Many of the classic revolutions in the history of science fall here. These include the elimination of the Aristotelian-Ptolemaic cosmology and the gastric theory of ulcers with the rise, respectively, of the Copernican theory and the bacterial theory (Thagard 1992, 1999).

New Wave reductionists, especially the Churchlands, famously argue that many cases of intertheoretic relations at the interface of psychology and neuroscience should be located at this end of the continuum as well. They contend that it will be the psychological theories, especially our folk psychology of beliefs and desires, that will end up on the scrap heap of the history of science, along with other discarded theories about such things as phlogiston, caloric fluid, the luminiferous ether and an expanding and contracting, but otherwise stable, Earth (P. S. Churchland 1986: 373; P. M. Churchland 1989: 1–22).

Such pronouncements rightfully transfix antireductionists, including those in religious studies, since, if the Churchlands' claims were true, they would suggest that antireductionists' claims in behalf of the religious, the meaningful, the spiritual, the subjective, the conscious, the experiential, the historical, the sociocultural, and the culturally constructed would probably face the same fate, even, perhaps, at the hands of the newly flourishing cognitive science of religion.

Although I do not mean to rule out absolutely the possibility of eliminating some cherished conceptions, long-deployed in religious studies, I do want to argue, first, that such upheavals would not arise according to the New Wavers' blueprint and, second, that a more satisfactory conception of cross-scientific relations, namely, explanatory pluralism, suggests (of a piece with the principle of evidential opportunism that I highlighted before) that the foremost form of interaction between the cognitive science of religion and traditional religious studies will be one of mutual enhancement.

What is wrong with the New Wavers' blueprint? New Wave models analyze theory succession over time within some science the same way that they analyze the relations of theories from different sciences at some particular point in time. In short, they ignore the differences between *successor* relations and *cross-scientific* relations. They are wont to ignore this distinction because the New Wave continuum *can* be deployed in *both* settings and cases arise in both in which the intertheoretic translations are abysmal. But it does not follow that the two settings involve the same dynamics.

Successor relations concern changes over time within a science at some level of analysis. As the New Wavers' continuum shows, the mapping of one reigning theory onto its successor can range from smooth to bumpy to no contact whatsoever, short of some overlap in their *explananda*. The changes during such theoretical transitions in some science can be minor or major; they can be gradual or abrupt. The alterations to the account of free fall near the surface of the Earth across the history of modern physical science have been minor and gradual. This is an example of scientific *evolution*. More recent and more *general* mechanical accounts can make sense of and improve upon the earlier notions of free fall. By contrast, when changes are major and abrupt, for example, the change from Stahl's account to Lavoisier's account of combustion, they constitute one of Kuhn's scientific *revolutions* (see Figure 1.3).

Other than the fact that they address many of the same aspects of the world, that is, that they have some common *explananda*, the theories in these cases have so few connections that the triumphant successor does not reductively explain its predecessor. Instead, it eliminates it. Across its history science has frequently discarded once-honored theories and large portions, if not all, of their ontologies, concerning everything from the crystalline spheres above to

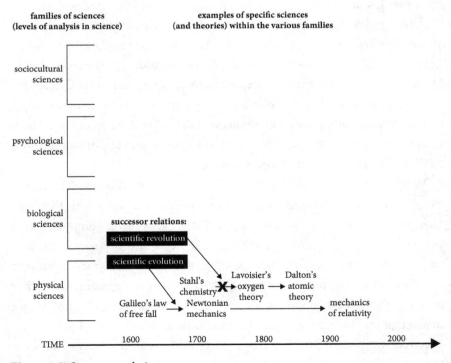

Figure 1.3 Successor relations.

the bodily humors within, in favor of new, superior successors. Eliminations can occur in either case, but whereas in the evolutionary settings, they only involve small parts of a theory and tinkering at their edges, in revolutionary settings they are overwhelming, if not complete. So, although most of Galileo's mechanical proposals, for example, his concept of inertia, can be plausibly mapped onto Newtonian mechanics, his notion of *natural motions*, which Galileo inherited (and transformed) from the ancients, falls away. By contrast, all of the principles and ontology of Stahl's chemistry are abandoned less than three decades after the publication of Lavoisier's new theory (Thagard 1992).

Cross-scientific relations concern arrangements of a very different sort. Cross-scientific relations are those between different sciences with a common *explanandum* operating simultaneously at different levels of analysis either within or across the families of the sciences. Everyone from molecular level neuroscientists all the way up to the highest level social scientists seek models for explaining aspects of human behavior and mentality. Evidential opportunism is not the only kind of opportunism in science. Scientists at any level will have a host of reasons to look to research carried out at another level, whether downstairs or upstairs. They may seek new forms of evidence, new experimental techniques and tools, or new theoretical resources. Scientists will borrow useful tools of any sort wherever they can be found. Often they are most easily found among other scientists approaching related problems at a different analytical level.

We call looking downstairs "reductionism." When inquirers discover a pattern among phenomena at one level, a standard explanatory strategy in science is to look downstairs for a mechanism responsible for that pattern. If psychologists find dissociations between people's abilities to locate an object and their abilities to identify that object, it is reasonable to look for separate processing streams for such information in the brain. Or if, across cultures, rituals overwhelmingly cluster around certain attractor positions in the space of possibilities, it is reasonable to look for underlying psychological mechanisms to explain the appeal of the corresponding forms (McCauley and Lawson 2002). Arguably, such reductionism has proved one of the most effective problem-solving strategies in the history of modern science.

As noted, the New Wavers' continuum of intertheoretic mapping can be applied in these cross-scientific contexts just as readily as it can in successor contexts. When the mapping is particularly good, the conditions approximate the logical empiricists' ideal, and the success of the reducing theory at the lower level generally *vindicates* the reduced theory. Physical accounts of atomic structure, for example, sustain the principles of molecular bonding in chemistry. Successful reductive explanation in cross-scientific settings does not supply grounds for replacing upper level theories and sciences. Rather, what it demonstrates is that in at least one limited area (specified by the boundary conditions that are incorporated either in the traditional model's bridge principles or in the implicit limits of the New Wavers' theory-analogue) the upper level theory's explanatory principles accurately and usefully summarize the myriad details of the microstructures and processes that the lower level account captures. Even though they are always context-specific, successful cross-scientific (approximate) reductions provide reasons for *retaining* not only the upper level theories but the research programs they inspire, the investigative tools they motivate, the evidence they generate and the ontologies they presume. One illustration of such cross-scientific cooperation is the neurosciences' widespread reliance on the theoretical resources, the experimental designs, and the empirical findings of experimental psychology (e.g., Hirst and Gazzaniga 1988: 276, 294, 304–305). Note that rather than explaining away or eliminating the upper level science or its theories, this is an instance of research in a lower level science (neuroscience) taking inspiration and obtaining aid from a higher level science (experimental psychology).

So, if the inter-level mapping is good between claims in religious studies about the religious, the meaningful, the spiritual, and so on and cognitive theories of religion, then there are not only no grounds for worrying about the elimination of religious studies' projects but there are also reasons to expect an ongoing cross-pollination between them and those of the cognitive scientists. This, however, is the easy case. What about cases when the connections between religious studies' prized notions and cognitive theories are meager?

Explanatory pluralism

Because they do not distinguish between successor and cross-scientific contexts, the New Wavers presume that substantial breakdowns of intertheoretic mapping will *always* end in the eradication of one of the theories in play. The elimination of scientific theories on the basis of cross-scientific comparisons that they envision could lead to the wholesale elimination of the *sciences* from which those theories issue. It would, after all, be forlorn to pursue some line of research dominated by a thoroughly discredited theory. At least some of the time (P. M. Churchland 1981; Bickle 1998: 205–206, 2003: 110), neither Churchland nor Bickle has retreated in the face of that apparent consequence of their views.

Explanatory pluralism maintains that when the connections between theoretical projects at different levels of analysis are fragmentary, the dynamics of cross-scientific relations differ from those between successive theories within some science (McCauley 1986a, 1996, 2009; McCauley and Bechtel 2001; Looren de Jong and Schouten 2007; Dale et al. 2009). If we can rule out the New Wavers' one-size-fits-all model of reduction, reductionist research strategies should no longer automatically sound alarms for scholars of religion.

With regard to cases of negligible intertheoretic mapping, the New Wavers' penchant for treating successor and cross-scientific cases the same does not square either with the historical illustrations they cite or with the principle of evidential opportunism (or with the broader opportunism) that characterizes scientific inquiries. Neither the historical evidence nor plausible conceptions of science suggest that the New Wavers' eliminativist conclusions in cross-scientific settings are sound.

The historical argument: the New Wavers identify no convincing cases from the history of science illustrating their claims for the possibility of eliminations in cross-scientific settings (McCauley 2007). *All* of the illustrations of theory eliminations in the history of science at which the New Wavers point (including the theories of the bodily humors, crystalline spheres, impetus, phlogiston, caloric fluid, the luminiferous ether, phrenological faculties, and vital spirits) have resulted from theory succession within a particular science. *None* of these eliminations have resulted from comparisons of theories in cross-scientific settings, that is, from the comparison of theories reigning simultaneously in sciences operating at different analytical levels, and, in particular, across the borders between the major families of sciences (see Figure 1.4). Scientific revolutions and the theoretical and ontological eliminations they underwrite occur between successive theories in some science, not between theories operating at different levels of analysis.

The normative argument: explanatory pluralism suggests that the New Wavers' putative cross-scientific eliminations would simply decrease the

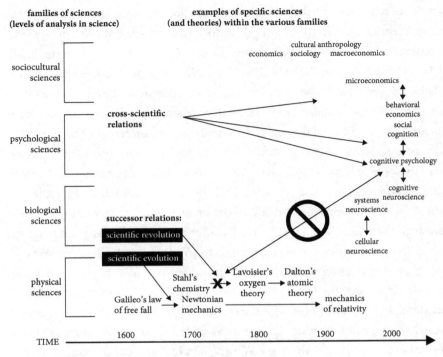

Figure 1.4 Cross-scientific vs. successor relations.

theoretical, evidential, and experimental resources available for science to call upon, and, thus, deprive it of resources for further testing theories. The sciences' honorific epistemic status depends in part on their ongoing demand for *new* empirical tests. Much of the evidence that a theory must account for stems from work at other (including higher) levels of analysis.

Contrary to the New Wave picture, explanatory pluralism stresses that cross-scientific pressures do not cause scientific disciplines to disappear, certainly not once they have achieved both intellectual stability based on theoretical and empirical accomplishments and institutional stability based on professional societies, specialized journals, and university departments. Their persistence increases the range of explanations that science furnishes and proffers empirical findings that, consistent with the principle of evidential opportunism, may abet research in other sciences.

Explanatory pluralism does not merely showcase the *reductionist* strategy for integrating the sciences. It also emphasizes the role of a *contextualist* strategy in which scientists use higher level sciences to explore the settings in which a system may be situated and the various external factors that constrain its shape, its inputs, and, therefore, its behaviors (see Craver 2007: 189). Scientists can just as readily look upstairs, exploring some targeted item's place and role in larger systems. They can examine the item's position in, and interactions with, its environment, and they can examine the contributions it makes to the characteristic patterns those larger systems exhibit.

Contrary to the special pleading of antireductionists for the autonomy of some inquiry or phenomenon, explanatory pluralism holds that exploring reductive possibilities downstairs, no less than exploring integrative contextualist possibilities upstairs, opens new avenues for sharing both explanatory insights and methodological, theoretical, and evidential resources. Antireductionists' special pleading not only forestalls the checks and balances that reductive integration imposes, it also blocks opportunities for new investigations at both levels and for collaborative research between them. Concerns for access to the full range of available evidence and problem-solving strategies will—at all levels of scientific inquiry—safeguard (rather than diminish) spaces for reductive explorations. The explanatory pluralist's message is that, unaccompanied by scientistic agendas, those spaces for reductive explorations pose no threats to research carried out at higher analytical levels or, more specifically, to the traditional programs of interpretive research in religious studies.

Explanatory pluralism also offers a rationale for why, with regard to the putative slings and arrows of reductionism, scholars in religious studies may, perhaps, have *less* to worry about than most antireductionists. After all, for more than a century, religious studies have often engaged research from across the sociocultural sciences (Durkheim [1915] 1965; Weber 1964) and the psychological sciences (James 1902/1929; Freud 1927/1961). Some scholars in religious studies (e.g., Burkert 1996) have even taken inspiration from the biological sciences, just as the new cognitive scientists of religion have. The point is that for decades religious studies have frequently functioned as an opportunistic enterprise, taking inspiration, in particular, from the highest levels of the social sciences, from the psychology of religion, and, in the case of Freud, even from the sub-personal psychological levels. The emerging cognitive science of religion facilitates explorations *downward* to new areas of sub-personal psychological research and, at least recently, down further to

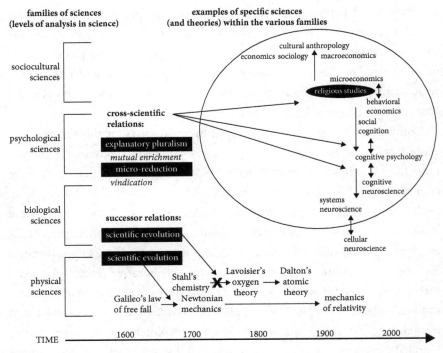

Figure 1.5 Explanatory pluralism.

the findings from the new imaging technologies in the neurosciences (e.g., Schjoedt et al. 2009) (see Figure 1.5).

Scholars of religion have seen firsthand that progress in the psychology of religion has not put the sociology or the anthropology of religion out of business, no more than the amazing progress of molecular neuroscience over the past three decades will put cognitive neuroscience or the psychology of religion out of business.

According to explanatory pluralism, any reductionist impulses exhibited by the cognitive science of religion exhibits only promise means for further enriching our understanding of the religious, the meaningful, the spiritual, and so on. The kinds of cross-scientific connections involved do not lead to the elimination of either fields (such as religious studies) or their objects of study.

A footnote: not even scientific revolutions between successive theories within a particular science typically involve the elimination of phenomena. To recognize the theories as competitors depends upon the substantial overlap of their *explananda*.

Two ways that the cognitive science of religion and traditional religious studies can be mutually enriching

On the basis of a variety of cognitive considerations, my and Tom Lawson's cognitive theory of participants' religious ritual competence draws a major distinction between two major classes of religious rituals (McCauley and Lawson 2002). One of those classes is "special agent rituals." Special agent rituals are those in which agents possessing counterintuitive properties ("CI-agents" hereafter) serve, either directly or via their ritually established intermediaries (e.g., priests), as the *agents* in participants' tacit cognitive representations of the rituals in question. In religious participants' commerce with the gods, special agent rituals are the religious rituals in which CI-agents do something to religious participants, at least some of whom, in any given case, serve as the patients of these rituals.

By virtue of their counterintuitive properties, CI-agents are capable of doing things *once and for all*. They need not repeat themselves. Consequently, participants typically need to participate in these special agents rituals as their patients only once. Participants typically are baptized only once, go through only one bar mitzvah, are wedded to their spouse only once, and so on. Participants may *observe* the various rites of passage and all other special agent rituals (consecrations, investitures, etc.) many times, but the patients of those special agent rituals will change with each performance.

Lawson and I have argued that it is by virtue of participants' cognitive representation of special agent rituals' forms that they incorporate comparatively elevated levels of sensory pageantry. High levels of sensory stimulation, either positive or negative, across any of the sensory modalities tend to excite human emotions and arouse human minds, which Lawson and I maintain is just the ticket for marking the personal and cultural salience of an event. By contrast, Harvey Whitehouse has, in effect, maintained that the high levels of sensory pageantry are a function of the comparative infrequency of special agent rituals' performance (Whitehouse 1995, 2004). All three of us agree, however, that special agent rituals inhabit a hotspot within the space of possible ritual arrangements, in which performance frequency is low and comparative levels of the sensory pageantry associated with such rituals is high (see Figure 1.6). We also agree that in combination with a variety of other

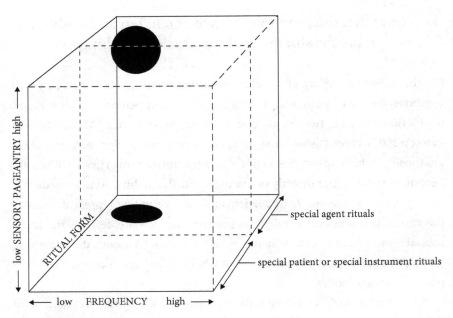

Figure 1.6 Special agent rituals.

factors, these rituals are likely to prove comparatively memorable, meaningful, and motivational. Here I wish to highlight that third feature.

Crucially, "motivation" here connotes, among other things, participants' inclinations to transmit their religious representations to others. Since such transmission is a necessary condition for a religion's growth, from the standpoint of cultural evolution these motivational effects of special agent rituals matter (Sosis and Alacorta 2003; Atran and Henrich 2010). A few complications aside (which Lawson and I address at length elsewhere), the more times a participant serves as the patient of a special agent ritual the more likely that participant will be to act on and transmit his or her religious representations (McCauley and Lawson 2002: 124–192; Ginges et al. 2009). That observation, though, occasions a dilemma.

The dilemma is that although it is an advantage for a religion to provide a steady regimen of special agent rituals, typically, as I have noted, participants serve as the patients of special agent rituals only once. Because of the expenses involved in producing the elevated levels of sensory pageantry associated with special agent rituals (including such things as special foods, clothing, music, and dance), having a large menu of *different* special agent rituals will quickly present prohibitively high costs. Consequently, there is an incentive for religions to have some means by which they can *repeat* a more limited list of special agent rituals with the *same* patients.

At least three sorts of ritually extraordinary circumstances permit the repetition of special agent rituals with the same ritual patients, namely, reversals, failures, and substitutions. If two people are divorced, they can be remarried. If the ritual practitioner performing the special agent ritual is an imposter, the performance is invalid and must be done again. If one person stands in for another, then that person may undergo a special agent ritual another time.

Substitution in special agent rituals is the best of these options for a host of reasons. Those reasons include negative considerations associated with the first two options having to do with risking the appearance either of fickleness, indifference, or impotence among the gods or of iniquity or incompetence among ritual practitioners. They also include positive considerations in addition to the fact that ritual substitution has none of the major disadvantages associated with the other two options. Among those positive considerations are that ritual substitution supplies both prospective and retrospective justifications for repeating a special agent ritual with the same patient and it affords a limitless number of such re-performances. No considerations of ritual form constrain the number of persons for which a participant can substitute.

Mutual enrichment: my and Lawson's theory of religious ritual competence not only discloses these social patterns but explains them on cognitive grounds. Having a theory that both ascertains these general patterns across religious systems and illuminates some of the dynamics underlying them certainly endows explanatory insights available to all scholars of religion, regardless of their methodological or theoretical orientations. That is one way the cognitive science of religion can enrich religious studies.

The question remains, however, whether this relatively idealized cognitive theorizing actually squares with the facts on the ground. The account I have sketched above generates at least one prediction, namely that, that, all else being equal, religions that allow the repeated substitution of the same ritual participants in special agent rituals will enjoy a competitive advantage over those that do not. Scholars of religion, especially historians of religion, can play a vital role here. The obvious questions are: what religions had or have such rituals and did they or do they enjoy such a competitive advantage? I do not wish to be coy here. In a separate paper I note one religion that does employ such ritual substitution and briefly sketch a case for the claim that, *ceteris paribus*, it does enjoy such a competitive advantage (McCauley 2012). Just identifying religions that have incorporated participants' substitution for patients in special agent rituals would be a valuable contribution. Presumably, no one is better prepared than historians of religion to report on the fate of those religions! That is one way in which religious studies can enrich the cognitive science of religion.

Cognitive scientists of religion welcome such collaboration.

2

Interpretation and Explanation: Problems and Promise in the Study of Religion

with E. Thomas Lawson

Introduction

Symbolic-cultural systems are a puzzlement. As forms of thought and types of behavior they seem bizarre. Why do the Dorze of Ethiopia say that the leopard is a Christian animal, which observes the fast days of the Orthodox Church while protecting their goats from marauding leopards on those same fast days? Why do the Yoruba of Nigeria think that marks on a divining board that a diviner makes and reads simultaneously disclose and determine their future? Why does a marriageable Zulu male regard it as more important to swallow a foul tasting potion to become attractive to an eligible young woman of his clan than simply relying on special adornment? Why do some Christians assert that bread and wine, once consecrated, become the body and blood of Jesus Christ?

Answering questions such as these requires metatheoretical, theoretical, and substantive reflection. A crucial metatheoretical thesis we wish to defend is that interpretive and explanatory endeavors need not be antagonistic and, in fact, should interact in the study of symbolic-cultural systems.

The continuing vigorous debate among social scientists and humanists about the roles that interpretation and explanation play in the analysis of human affairs (and the extremeness of the positions that some adopt) should rapidly eliminate any doubt about the importance of this metatheoretical question for inquiries into symbolic-cultural systems. Most scholars agree that this issue is both serious and unavoidable. They differ widely, however, not only in their views of the relationships between interpretation and explanation but also about the contents of the terms. Still, most do agree that interpretation involves questions of meaning and that explanation concerns causal relations (in some sense).

Proponents of the extreme positions maintain either that symbolic-cultural systems are only susceptible to interpretation (and not explanation) or that they are susceptible to explanation (and interpretation is irrelevant). The language they use frequently frames the pertinent issues in exclusivistic terms. On the one hand, scientistic thinkers (influenced by logical empiricism) read interpretive approaches as unduly subjective and personal, as speculations without foundation, and as deflecting inquiry from its true purposes—which are to produce law-like causal explanations of human behavior. On the other hand, hermeneuticists regard such scientistic views both as mechanistic (or "reductionistic") descriptions which are insensitive to the role that the investigator's subjectivity, values, and biases play in the pursuit of knowledge and as naive approaches which fail to appreciate the importance of questions of meaning for our understanding of human life and thought. The issue separating these feuding factions is whether or not the subject matter of the human sciences is privileged, hence requiring special categories and methods. Those of scientistic bent argue that no subject matter is privileged, that science is a unified enterprise, and that the only kind of knowledge worth pursuing is that which is produced by the kinds of methods the physical sciences employ. Those with hermeneutic inclinations fight for a privileged status for both subject matter and method and accuse those of scientistic bent of physics envy.

While the appeal to a privileged status for method and subject matter in the human sciences is widespread, it is particularly strong in the thought of those scholars involved in the study of religion and in the history of religions in particular. That field manifests a serious imbalance in favor of interpretation over explanation. For example, Eliade (1963: xiii) says:

> A religious phenomenon will only be recognized as such if it is grasped at its own level, that is to say, if it is studied *as* something religious. To try to grasp the essence of such a phenomenon by means of physiology, psychology, sociology, economies, linguistics, art or any other study is false; it misses the one unique and irreducible element in it—the element of the sacred.

Eliade, here, is asserting that religious phenomena are *sui generis* and that they can be "grasped" (understood, interpreted) only if we grant to the category of "the sacred" a unique and irreducible status. From this point of view, explanatory theory, as developed in the social sciences, simply misses the crucial point, namely, that "the sacred" is accessible only by special (interpretive) techniques. In other words, the privileged status of the subject matter requires a special method—hermeneutics.

Eliade's protectionism is not an isolated case. The theologian Rudolf Otto (1958: 8), who had profound influence on the development of the history of religions as a separate discipline, claimed:

> The reader is invited to direct his mind to a moment of deeply-felt religious experience, as little as possible qualified by other forms of consciousness. Whoever cannot do this, whoever knows no such moments in his experience, is requested to read no farther; for it is not easy to discuss questions of religious psychology with one who can recollect the emotions of his adolescence, the discomforts of indigestion, or say, social feelings, but cannot recall any intrinsically religious feelings.

From Otto's point of view, interpretation of religious phenomena not only excludes explanation but *both presumes and requires* a prior religious experience. Hans Penner (1986) has argued that Otto's appeal to a privileged status for religious experience is theologically motivated and continues to be an unacknowledged assumption in methodological discussions in the history of religions—even when it is explicitly denied!

Examples such as these from the field of the history of religions could be multiplied but would serve little purpose. Our goal is not to excoriate historians of religions but to show that acknowledging the issues which preoccupy them does not require defending the antiscientific positions most adopt. In fact, we would be derelict in our duty if we did not also acknowledge that the pervasive emphasis on interpretation in the history of religions has encouraged deep sensitivity to the semantic complexities of religious systems and to the diversity and richness of religious forms of experience. Unfortunately, its neglect of explanation has left it bereft of systematic power and prone to highly individualist accounts of religious phenomena.

In addition to historians of religions, many scholars in the larger world of the social sciences and the humanities have taken the development of such sensitivities to the complexities of symbolic-cultural systems as a principled ground for preferring interpretation over explanation. Their views are typically rooted not, as in the history of religions, in claims about the privileged status of "the holy" or "the sacred," but in more extravagant claims about the autonomy of human behavior generally. Their view is that symbolic-cultural systems by their very nature require interpretive rather than explanatory approaches.

By contrast, we hold that interpretation and explanation are complementary and, in light of the imbalance within the study of religion in favor of interpretation that we wish to redress, the proposal of explanatory theories is more likely to advance our knowledge currently.

In the next section, we shall first describe the most prominent positions that have been advanced in the relevant literature concerning the relationship between interpretation and explanation. We think that both scientistic and hermeneutic hegemonists are wrong for claiming that the choices are *between* explanation and interpretation. Nor do we think that explanation is subordinate to interpretation. A more balanced position is not only possible but desirable.

Explanation and interpretation: Three accounts

When we are dealing with human subjects, their forms of thought, their types of practice, what are the respective roles of explanation and interpretation, however finely or coarsely they are distinguished? We think that a careful analysis of the debate discloses three views about how they are related. These are the actually occurring options in the literature as opposed to the much larger number of logically possible positions. The first are the *exclusive* positions to which we have already referred. Both hold that interpretation and explanation exclude one another. Their differences concern which of the two they favor. The second is the *inclusive*, which maintains that explanation is and must be subordinated to interpretation. Inclusivists hold that the enterprise of interpretation always encapsulates explanatory pursuits. The third, which we shall defend, is the *interactive*. It proposes that interpretation and explanation inform each other. Novel interpretations employ the categories of theories already in place, whereas novel explanations depend upon the discovery of new theories which, in turn, depends upon the sort of reorganization of knowledge that interpretive pursuits involve. On the interactive view, these two processes complement one another. We shall discuss each of these positions in order.

Exclusivism

The exclusivist positions are both hegemonic views. Exclusivism takes two forms, one emphasizing the centrality of explanation, the other the centrality of interpretation. The first group of exclusivists, consisting of behavioral psychologists, sociobiologists, and others, holds that the only methods for systematic inquiry are the methods of the natural sciences (see, for example, Skinner 1953: 87–90; Rosenberg 1980). The second, which focuses on interpretation exclusively, includes such postmodernist philosophers as Rorty (1982: 199) and holds that *all* inquiry is ultimately interpretive.

(1) For the first group, explanation excludes interpretation because human thought and behavior should be studied, like anything else in the world, according to the strict canons of scientific investigation modeled after inquiry in the physical sciences. Interpretation is irrelevant, if not impossible, for such purposes. Explanation is simply scientific explanation. On this exclusivist view, if the human sciences aspire to be sciences at all, then they should be modeled after the physical sciences. Both should search for causal laws which describe the behavior of the objects in their respective domains. Interpretive factors simply get in the way and introduce needless obscurities. For example, concerns with subjectivity or intentionality only interfere with scientific progress (Rosenberg 1980).

This position was most forcefully developed in the heyday of the logical empiricist philosophy of science. However, its influence has persisted. Richard Rudner's discussion (1966) of the philosophy of social science is a fitting illustration. Rudner maintained that the structure of theories in the study of social and cultural systems should mirror the idealized accounts of theories in the physical sciences that earlier logical empiricists had offered. For Rudner, understanding social worlds (just as understanding the natural world) is essentially a consequence of formulating causal explanations.

More recently, Adolf Grunbaum (1984) has taken up this banner in his attack on recent hermeneutical reinterpretations of Freud by Habermas,

Ricoeur, and Klein. For instance, Ricoeur, according to Grunbaum, reduces the object of psychoanalytic theory to the verbal transactions between psychoanalyst and patient and then argues that such verbal transactions require interpretive rather than explanatory approaches. Ricoeur, for example, says, "There are no 'facts' nor any observation of 'facts' in psychoanalysis but rather the interpretation of a narrated history" (1974: 186). Grunbaum argues that such a hermeneutic explication of psychoanalysis as interpretation rather than explanation conforms neither to the intention of Freud nor to the logical structure of his arguments. He argues that psychoanalysis, according to Freud, has the status of a natural science, in virtue of the fact that on Freud's view psychoanalysis proposes law-like generalizations to explain human behavior. Ironically, Grunbaum salvages the explanatory intent of Freudian psychoanalysis in order to scuttle it on different grounds, namely its "genuine epistemic defects, which are often quite subtle" (1984: xii) but which boil down to psychoanalysis' masking a crucial ambiguity about the role that suggestion plays in the psychoanalyst-patient relationship. Clearly, from Grunbaum's point of view, natural science is fundamentally explanatory and includes interpretive elements only incidentally. If psychoanalysis is to be a social *science*, then it should be modeled upon the natural sciences. There is no need to introduce interpretive categories.

What should be noted in this brand of exclusivism is how hermeneuticists such as Ricoeur play right into the hands of the scientistic exclusivists by acknowledging the right of the latter to establish the form and limits of explanation. For example, it is clear from the quotation taken from Ricoeur's work that he concedes to the logical empiricist the "observation of facts" which he then *contrasts* with narrative interpretation. He attempts to purchase autonomy for interpretation at the expense of its ability to contribute to explanation. Not surprisingly, as we shall see next, one form of exclusivism breeds another. Scientistic exclusivism leads to the hermeneutic variety, because it so limits acceptable subject matters and methods that it forces dissenters in response to focus upon just those features of human experience that extreme scientism ignores, such as the affective, the personal, the subjective, the meaningful, the valuable, and the imaginative, to name the most important.

(2) For the second group, interpretation excludes the possibility of explaining human behavior, because all inquiry about human life and thought

occurs within the ineliminable frameworks of values and subjectivity. This version of the exclusivity thesis is the mirror image of the first position and was partially developed in response to it. In this view human beings are subjects not objects; therefore, we should explicate the *meaning* of their thoughts and actions, rather than the alleged causal factors that account for their behavior. Human science reveals its differences from natural science by paying attention to a world of meanings rather than a system of causes. Its approach must be semiotic rather than nomological.

While such a semiotic approach has many exemplars in the human sciences (e.g., Lesche 1985), Clifford Geertz (in, at least, some of his moments) has been particularly influential in its defense. While his actual work contains a great deal of creative explanatory theorizing, his methodological pronouncements often have a decidedly exclusivistic ring. We should state at the outset that Geertz's pronouncements about these issues do not *always* follow along the lines we discuss here. Nevertheless, Geertz does enunciate this methodological perspective quite forthrightly in the following passage (1973: 5):

> The concept of culture I espouse and whose utility I now attempt to demonstrate is essentially a semiotic one. Believing with Max Weber, that man is an animal suspended in webs of significance he himself has spun, I take culture to be those webs, and the analysis of it to be, therefore, not an experimental science in search of law but an interpretive one in search of meaning.

Geertz, *here*, clearly advances an exclusivistic hermeneutic agenda; it is the job of the scholar in the human sciences to *interpret* the semiotic patterns of those "webs of significance" spun by humankind rather than to explain their connections. Interpretation does not mean proposing principles that show systematic connections among idealized theoretical objects, nor does it mean identifying causal factors; it means unpacking meanings. Human science should involve the *discernment* of meanings rather than the discovery of laws. A cultural system consists of "socially established structures of meaning." Because it is *socially* established, that is, a creation of the participants, it does not exist as an entity available for explanation. The only option is for the interpreter to enter it as a world of meaning. The interpreter is in the position of a stranger invited into a home or a reader enticed into reading a book. Explanatory theory is simply not to the point. This methodological perspective is not simply a heuristic strategy in the face of cultural complexity, but a necessary consequence of the character of human interaction—especially interaction across cultures.

Geertz sometimes seems to think that a principled ground exists for justifying the exclusive preference for interpretation in the study of human subjects in their self-woven cultural webs. The alleged problem lies in the very nature of explanation itself. It is not simply that it has a limited value nor that whatever explanations we do come across constrain our interpretations, but rather that our reading of cultural "texts" requires sensitivities to the subjective and semantic dimensions of human thought and action which are absent from explanatory approaches. On this position *the search for explanatory theories with respect to human subjects is fundamentally misdirected*. It fails to acknowledge the autonomy, independence, and uniqueness of the subject matter of the human sciences.

When pursuing this position, Geertz's argument goes something like the following: an examination of the practices of anthropologists (those scholars most directly involved with examining symbolic-cultural systems) discloses their fundamentally *ethnographic* approach. What ethnographers do is establish rapport with their subjects. They enter into a hermeneutic relationship with them. In such a relationship, they are consistently trying to understand other forms of human meaning. These other forms are not transparent to the ethnographer; their opaqueness requires interpretation. They need to be broken through. Geertz argues that such interpretive analysis involves "sorting out the structures of signification and determining their social ground and import" (Geertz 1973: 9). Questions of "import" are questions of interpretation which enlarge the universe of human discourse (1973: 14). Geertz thinks that the mistake made by those scholars who search for explanations is that they view culture as a power—something causally responsible for social events, behaviors, institutions, and processes. Instead, he thinks that a cultural system is a context, something within which the structures of signification can be "intelligibly—that is, thickly—described" (1973: 14).

With such views of culture and of the aim of anthropology there seems little, if any, room for explanatory theory. Interpretation, characterized now as thick description, in the context of the human universe of discourse is all that is possible. Ethnography as the interpretation of cultures excludes explanation. It must stay "much closer to the ground"; in fact, it is incapable of either generalization or prediction (1973: 24–26). Explanation is a matter for the "hard sciences." Ethnography, by its very nature, carves out an exclusive niche for itself, free from a concern with testable generalizations.

By now it should be clear that both forms of exclusivism are in remarkable agreement on at least two issues, namely (1) that explanation is the search for causes and the laws that describe their operation and (2) that the goals and methods of the natural sciences differ radically from our other knowledge-seeking activities. However, they draw exactly opposite conclusions (McCauley 1986b). The advocates of the explanatory methods of the physical sciences regard interpretive projects as *superfluous* speculations, whereas the advocates of the centrality of interpretation in the human sciences regard these endeavors as indispensable and explanatory projects as foreign and even inimical to understanding human affairs. They disagree only on whether causes and laws are applicable to human thought and action.

We think that the issues of relating explanation and interpretation are much more complex than the defenders of either of these exclusivistic positions willingly acknowledge. More moderate positions are clearly possible.

Inclusivism

The second and more moderate set of views is inclusive but still requires the *subordination* of explanation to interpretation. Although in principle inclusivism could be a two-way street, in fact, it is not. Reliably, it is explanation that is subordinated to interpretation and not the other way around. Such subordination takes a number of possible forms. We shall first discuss three versions of this view. We shall criticize a number of their common assumptions directly in the last part of this section and indirectly in the presentation of the interactionist position which follows.

(1) The first way of subordinating explanation to interpretation involves not so much the goals of inquiry as much as it does explanation's *practical* unrealizability. This view holds that the barriers to explanation in human matters are practical rather than principled. We may dub this approach "pragmatic modesty" and Edward Shils (1972) is its best representative. He willingly acknowledges the lack of nomological progress in the human sciences

and thinks that practitioners in the human sciences cannot do much more at present than set their sights on more modest accomplishments. Perhaps one day the methods, procedures, and concepts of the social sciences will be more sophisticated and refined enough to place social and cultural inquiry on a firmer methodological and theoretical footing. But for now the human sciences are a "heterogeneous aggregate of topics, related to each other by a common name, by more or less common techniques, by a community of key words and conceptions, by a more or less commonly held aggregate of major interpretive ideas and schemas" (1972: 275). Interpretation is primary; explanation is subordinate.

According to Shils, human beings living in social situations have had to make policy decisions for millennia. The practicalities of such decision making lead to questions about the principles on which they are made, that is, the basis for choosing one policy rather than another for organizing and enhancing social life. What is the basis for those policies which guide human choices? "Social science" simply makes this complex and intricate project of devising adequate and fruitful policy for the ordering of social life more systematic. It is an essentially interpretive undertaking driven by the practical necessities of life. It is not that interpretation excludes explanation; explanation is allowable but, at present, unreachable. That is not where we need to place our attention.

Shils states his position most forcefully in the following passage (1972: 275–276):

> Most sociology is not scientific. It contains little of generality of scope and little of fundamental importance which is rigorously demonstrated by commonly accepted procedures for making relatively reproducible observations of important things. Its theories are not ineluctably bound to its observations. The standards of proof are not stringent. Despite valiant efforts its main concepts are not precisely defined; its most interesting interpretive propositions are not unambiguously articulated.

So, whereas social science is not very scientific in terms of rigorous demonstration, reproducible results, and all the other paraphernalia that accompany natural sciences, as a system of interpretation, "an aggregate of major interpretive ideas and schemes" constraining a severely limited explanatory component it is capable of effecting human progress.

(2) Some scholars argue that, in the case of human subjects, understanding is not only the *goal* of inquiry in the human sciences but must also be the *method* of inquiry. When human symbolic systems are the subject matter of study explanatory approaches cannot reach the goal of understanding without first adverting to the rational content of the systems in need of explication and rational content requires rational analysis. The consequence of that view is that reasons require understanding and not causal explication. The human sciences study reasons rather than causes because human action is, in fact, behavior undergirded by reasons. Reasons require understanding and therefore interpretation; causes require explanation. According to Peter Winch (1958: 23), Durkheim adopted a regressive position when he said:

> I consider extremely fruitful this idea that social life should be explained, not by the notions of those who participate in it, but by more profound causes which are unperceived by consciousness, and I think that these causes are to be sought mainly in the manner according to which the associated individuals are grouped. Only in this way, it seems, can history become a science, and sociology itself exist.

As Winch recognizes, Durkheim is trying to establish a social science according to the model of a natural science by attempting to locate "more profound causes" than rational contents which are normally held to explain human behavior. From Durkheim's point of view, the ideas of the members of a society are not the subject matter of the social sciences; that subject matter about which scientific generalizations can and should be made are "social relations."

Winch thinks that changing the subject matter in this way is a mistake and proposes, instead, that we look precisely at actions which are performed for reasons. When we analyze such actions we uncover meaningful behavior. "All behavior which is meaningful (therefore all specifically human behavior) is *ipso facto* rule-governed" (1958: 52). Such rule-governed behavior has more to do with the relationships between ideas requiring interpretation than it does with causal relationships involving theoretical explanation. "It is like applying one's knowledge of a language in order to understand a conversation rather than like applying one's knowledge of the laws of mechanics to understand the workings of a watch" (1958: 183).

What is interesting about Winch's view is that it does not necessarily exclude the causal role that reasons might play in accounting for human behavior. After all, reasons can be causes. But Winch is more interested in analyzing the *relations* between reasons than their causal role. *Relations* between reasons and actions require an analysis in terms of rules rather than an explanation in terms of causes.

Winch's view has attracted ample criticism already (Wilson 1970). In addition, a more sophisticated version of the view has emerged. The reservations we express with Rudolf Makkreel's view discussed below apply with even greater force to the position Winch defends.

(3) Makkreel (1985) asserts that all discussions of human interests and intentions are *fundamentally* interpretive and that, virtually by definition, human interests and intentions pervade all human activity. Hence, as Rorty and other interpretive exclusivists have maintained, even the natural sciences contain an ineliminable interpretive element. However, there is a second sort of higher level, hermeneutic endeavor which recognizes the importance of subjects' *own* views of their interests and intentions, maintaining that they always constitute an additional set of factors which enter in the mix. Although these self-perceptions enjoy no ultimate explanatory privilege, they are also ineliminable in discussions of human affairs. Such interpretive endeavors set the agenda for any explanatory excursions we may make in our attempts to account for human behavior. This position is not antagonistic to explanation, but it does insist that explanatory projects are always dependent upon and, therefore, subordinated to the interpretive enterprise.

Makkreel states that "explanation involves subsuming the particular data or elements that can be abstracted from our experience under general laws, whereas understanding is more concerned with focusing on the concrete contents of individual processes of experience to consider how they function as part of a *larger continuum*" (1985: 238, emphasis ours). He thinks that any understanding of human experience will have to subordinate explanatory theories (which are arrived at by *abstraction*) to interpretive endeavors (which are focused on the concrete contents of that human experience). These concrete contents have a priority over abstractions from human experience. Furthermore, the point about these contents of experience is not so much what accounts for them as it is their position and role in the "larger continuum."

Makkreel does not shrink from the charge of circularity so frequently leveled at hermeneuticists. In fact, he acknowledges the circularity of hermeneutics and argues that it is productive. Its productivity lies in its ability to "widen our framework of interpretation and generate new meaning, so that we will not just refine our original understanding but enrich it" (1985: 247).

Although we thoroughly concur with Makkreel's view of the productivity of interpretation, the position he defends seems incomplete at certain points. Happily, his view widens the hermeneutic circle by focusing on the production of new meaning. But it faces three problems. First, the production of new meaning assumes a great deal of background knowledge (which is both relatively fixed and relatively reliable). Both the fixity and reliability of that background knowledge depend largely upon the stability of previously established explanatory theories. Consequently, the hermeneutical process presupposes, in part, what it allegedly subordinates. The point, in short, is that we cannot expand our meanings without already assuming that we have some knowledge of the world already in place.

Second, the position in question does not deny the possibility of empirical psychology. Presumably, some theories in that field constitute part of the background knowledge which undergirds interpretations. The world that science discloses includes facts about ourselves. Consequently, the priority attributed to self-perceptions of interests and intentions is problematic in the face of scientific findings to the contrary. For example, considerable recent work in social cognition has consistently demonstrated subjects' ready willingness to cite plausible common-sense explanations of their behaviors in terms of standard folk accounts of their interests and intentions, even when, unbeknownst to them, those accounts are thoroughly unrelated to the causal variables experimenters have isolated which are sufficient to explain the overwhelming bulk of the variance in their behaviors (see Nisbett and Wilson 1977; Nisbett and Ross 1980; Stich 1983; Churchland 1986). In light of this research, it is unclear why researchers should hold out for the ineliminable importance of subjects' accounts of their intentions and interests in *all* cases of intentional action.

These self-attributions are informed by our prevailing common-sense view in psychology. But the history of science is replete with examples of new scientific discoveries overthrowing the prevailing common-sense or folk theories. Common sense is theoretical through and through (Churchland 1979). This includes not only common-sense views of the external world but also common-sense views of (even our own) internal, psychological goings-on (Churchland 1988). If common-sense accounts can compete with those of science, then they are subject to correction or even elimination in light of the theoretical upheavals which characterize scientific change (McCauley 1986a).

Third, although the production of new meaning may enrich our knowledge, it cannot account for the production of new *knowledge*. At least some of the time when the world proves recalcitrant to the theories that we propose, neither the stock of meanings we possess nor the interpretations we impose are capable of overcoming the disparity. Rappaport (1979: 139) protests that "as law cannot do the work of meaning neither can meaning do the work of law. The lawful operation of natural processes is neither constituted nor transformed by understanding, and the laws of nature prevail in their domains whether or not they are understood or meaningful." Occasionally, phenomena from the parts of the world that our established theories organize refuse to behave properly no matter how much those theories bend. Every genuinely *empirical* theory has its breaking point, and the incompatibility of some phenomena is too heavy for them to bear. If they could accommodate anything, the theories in question would not be empirical. Although Kuhn (1970), Laudan (1977), and others have documented the many strategies scientists have employed to shelve such anomalies, they concede that in the long run it is precisely the persistence and proliferation of such anomalies that is the single most fundamental force in scientific change. If all theories could accommodate anything (by simply producing new meanings), we could make no sense whatsoever of distinguishing between the relative empirical responsibility of the various disciplines such that it remains uncontroversial when we label some as sciences.

Hence, the development of new explanatory theories has one foot in the hermeneutical circle but another outside it as well, at least to the extent that we *presume* a great deal of explanatory knowledge when we contemplate alternative interpretations. This is not to say that interpretation has no role here, but rather that in any inquiry we *must* leave the huge majority of our systematic empirical knowledge unquestioned. Inquiry could not proceed if we left even much of that knowledge up for grabs. Certainly, the generation of new explanatory knowledge does depend, in part, on interpretive endeavors, whose production of new meanings is an important step in that process. It refines and enriches our conceptual resources from which new theoretical proposals emerge. However, that the generation of new theory depends upon the production of new meanings does not imply that explanatory knowledge is uniquely subordinate in some fundamental way to the interpretive enterprise. Indeed, we are suggesting that interpretive pursuits presuppose and, thus, depend just as surely on explanatory knowledge.

Consequently, we maintain that the growth of knowledge depends upon the *interaction* of interpretation and explanation. Widening the circle of meanings is not enough. A satisfactory epistemology must make sense of both the recent psychological findings which bear on our folk theories about the way the mind works and the distinction between scientific and nonscientific pursuits. Still, Makkreel's concern with the problem of understanding the role of individual elements within a larger conceptual system is important. The point, however, is that questions of meaning do not exhaust questions of knowledge. It is our view that both hermeneutic exclusivists and the various inclusivist versions of the relationships between interpretation and explanation have conceded more than they should to the logical empiricists' account of natural science and to their account of scientific explanation in particular. Therefore, they have adopted unduly defensive positions about the relative autonomy (indeed, the priority!) of interpretation and unnecessarily circumscribed the territory in which they think the human sciences can make substantial progress. In our discussion of interactionism, we shall suggest that logical empiricism is not nearly as intimidating as it might appear.

Interactionism

The third position, which we call the interactive, neither excludes nor subordinates. It acknowledges the differences between interpretation and explanation and champions the positive values of each. We do not think that explanation is free from interpretive elements. On the contrary, explanation is riddled with interpretation. Nor do we think that interpretation either can or should supplant or supersede explanation, even in the study of human subjects. The temptation to think that it could (to which both hermeneutic exclusivism and inclusivism succumb) is based, in large part, upon overwhelming attention to the model of explanation promoted by the paradigmatic explanatory exclusivists, namely, the logical empiricists. Their attention to the logical empiricist model of explanation has blinded hermeneutic exclusivists and inclusivists to relevant work in recent philosophy of science and psychology. The exclusivist and inclusivist approaches we have discussed fail to appreciate the positive contributions that both interpretation and explanation make in creating understanding.

In the remainder of this chapter, we shall briefly examine the general philosophical issues and present a less rigid view of explanation. We begin, however, with a short discussion of the logical empiricist model of explanation and some problems it faces.

Over the last twenty years, philosophers of science have thoroughly criticized the model of scientific explanation which the logical empiricists advanced (Suppe 1977). That model focused quite selectively on the *logical features* of explanations in the physical sciences. The logical empiricists' preoccupation with the *physical sciences* was a function of their covert metaphysical agenda and those sciences' rigor and success (Oppenheim and Putnam 1958). Their preoccupation with logical issues was a function of the power and clarity that prior achievements in logic offered for the analysis of claims and the logical empiricists' larger epistemological project which was a version of Cartesian foundationalism with a decidedly empiricist twist.

Their project was foundational, since they maintained that our only justifiable knowledge consisted in the truths of logic and those claims that survived the rigors of empirical verification. Claims which could not be empirically tested must be translatable into those which could. Such translation depended upon ultimately explicating all non-logical notions in terms of some observable predicate or other. This process, which included the reduction of the theoretical to the observable, promised logical empiricism a thoroughly extensional semantics. The logical empiricists confined knowledge to the logically and empirically knowable, and they confined the meaningful to the knowable so defined. On this view, then, the formal and physical sciences are not only the paradigms of human knowledge, they may well exhaust it. Other sorts of human utterances—the poetic, the moral, the political, the metaphysical, and the religious were expressive at best or, more often, utter nonsense.

The logical empiricists held that scientists explain phenomena when they have formulated theories that employ true causal laws which in conjunction with statements of initial and boundary conditions suffice as the premises of a deductive argument from which a statement about the phenomenon to be explained follows as a deductive consequence. The phenomenon to be explained is the *explanandum* and the laws and the statement about conditions from which the explanandum is derived constitute the *explanans*. On this view, explanation is both deductive and nomological. Explanations which conform to the deductive-nomological (or D-N) model utilize "covering" laws which have the form of universally quantified conditional statements. Such laws claim that for *all* objects, *if* certain initial and boundary conditions obtain, *then* the phenomenon to be explained will as well. The statements in the explanans about the relevant conditions assert that they have, indeed, obtained, so the explanandum follows as the conclusion of a straightforward deductive argument (Hempel 1965).

Critics have objected to nearly every aspect of the logical empiricist program. We will not rehearse all of those criticisms here. Before we briefly discuss some problems with their D-N (or covering law) model of explanation in particular, we will simply list five internal problems with the logical empiricists' epistemology which, even most of them recognized, had utterly resisted satisfactory solution (see, for example, Carnap 1936–1937). This is not to imply that these five points exhaust logical empiricism's weaknesses or problems.

(1) The distinction between theory and observation was pivotal to logical empiricism. It tracked a further distinction between the empirical foundation of knowledge and the theoretical edifice constructed upon it. Unfortunately, as yet no one has satisfactorily formulated either distinction and subsequent research seems to indicate that no one is ever likely to, since evidence mounts from a number of quarters that we make few, if any, observations independently of a theoretical framework (Brown 1979; Churchland 1979).

(2) Even if they could have forged an acceptable distinction between theory and observation, it became obvious early on that the meaning of most theoretical terms was not exhaustively reducible to observational

terms and certainly not by means of the mechanisms that the first-order predicate calculus afforded. They could accomplish very partial reductions, at best. This jeopardized the logical empiricists' goal of developing a thoroughly extensional semantics (and undermined their dismissive view of nonscientific discourse).

(3) Although they rarely singled out the foundational claims of their own position for derision, the logical empiricists' theses on meaning and truth (in particular) failed, just as thoroughly as the most speculative metaphysical claims, to satisfy their own criteria for meaningfulness and truth (see Putnam 1981: 103–126, 1981: 184–204).

(4) Their confidence in science notwithstanding, logical empiricists never offered a convincing solution to the logical problem of induction. For the logical empiricists, the premier attraction of science resided in the verification of laws of nature. However, they could not supply adequate grounds to justify their confidence in those laws' truth, since scientific laws are, indeed, conditional claims which apply *universally* (Popper 1972).

(5) Finally, logical empiricism propounded a normative view of science which excluded many of the sciences! Not only did most of the sciences substantially differ from the idealized model of physical inquiry the logical empiricists championed, some critics suggested that even areas of physical inquiry failed to meet its exacting standards. Probably logical empiricism's most off-putting consequence on this count was its failure to make sense of much of the work in the biological sciences and in the development of the synthetic theory of evolution, in particular. The rigor of their model of scientific explanation came at a heavy price.

These last two points bear directly on problems with the deductive-nomological model of explanation. Item (4) concerned the problem of establishing the truth of universally quantified claims which is one version of the problem of induction. The D-N model of explanation requires not only that scientific explanations use laws but also that those laws are true. Logical empiricism never offered any suitable means for ascertaining how we could ever know that proposed scientific laws met this criterion.

Item (5) discussed how the rigor of the logical empiricists' demands on acceptable science ended up excluding many activities that seemed clearly scientific. Their commitment to the D-N model of explanation also led to profound skepticism among the logical empiricists about those sciences' modes of explanation as well. Consequently, many critics have suggested that the D-N model of explanation is too rigid, when it requires, for example, that an explanation should be "logically conclusive" in the sense that it must offer a sound argument in support of the explanandum (Hempel 1965: 234). Even Hempel recognized that the stringency of this condition disqualified statistical and functional explanations in biology and psychology. In later work, he proposed accounts of both as the sorts of logical compromises (relative to the standards of the D-N model) which the complexities of some phenomena seem, at least presently, to demand. (Hempel 1965 discusses functional explanation [pp. 297–350], statistical explanation [pp. 376–412], and other forms of explanation which fall short of the D-N standards [pp. 412–489].)

Many critics, however, maintain that Hempel has not conceded enough and have suggested that these and other "corrupted" forms of scientific explanation are, in fact, the standard forms that scientists employ and, hence, ought to inspire proposed criteria for the acceptability of explanations in science (see, for example, Salmon 1970; Wimsatt 1972; McMullin 1978). Their general complaint is that the restrictiveness of the D-N model is not only excessive but is rather artificial as well. It captures neither the everyday nor the scientific sense of "explanation." The general consensus is that a science that confined itself to finding sound deductive-nomological explanations would make very little progress.

Ironically, other critics have argued that the D-N model of explanation is not demanding enough. In a now classic article, Bromberger (1966) found the D-N model too weak. The D-N model offers no apparatus for capturing the relation between the problems scientists face and the explanations they seek. The height of a pole can be deduced from information about the length of its shadow, the height of the sun, and a few geometrical and optical principles, but such a D-N account would hardly qualify as an *explanation* of the pole's height nor would it justify any causal attributions. Although Hempel claims that "in no other way than by reference to empirical laws can the assertion of a causal connection between events be scientifically substantiated" (1965: 233), Bromberger's charge, in short, is that the D-N model still does not supply sufficient conditions for a causal explanation.

This objection is of a piece with those of pragmatically oriented critics who charge that the logical empiricists' overwhelming concentration on the logical structure of finished theories and on the context of justification blinded them to considerations of practical problem solving and the role of discovery in scientific research (see, for example, Laudan 1977). According to these critics, logical empiricism was unduly taken with the formal, synchronic, and explanatory issues which questions of justification raised about finished theories in the physical sciences. It was, by contrast, almost completely silent on the practical, historical, and problem-solving issues which questions of discovery raise about the production of solutions not only to those theoretical problems but to technological, social, and (even) metaphysical ones as well. If not so obviously in the context of justification, certainly in the context of discovery *interpretive* questions resurface. Our suggestion is that even if scholars could draw a neat distinction between the contexts of justification and discovery, they are not fruitfully considered in isolation from one another. It is with such pragmatic considerations in mind that we offer (in contrast to the rigidity of the logical empiricist account) a less formal, general account of explanation in science. Before we take this project up, though, we need to comment on the multifarious character of explanation.

Explanatory concerns play a fundamental role in everyday life. Common sense provides the various explanatory principles to which we appeal in these everyday contexts. This collection of principles constitutes a rather diverse lot concerning both human behavior and natural phenomena. (The tails of friendly dogs wag; too many cooks spoil the broth; beggars can't be choosers; the sun rises in the east and sets in the west; a red sky at night is a sailor's delight; and so on.) The focus is on explaining *particular* events that occur in the course of everyday life, *usually in service to the interpretation of those events*. The fund of what we have called common-sense explanatory principles that are concerned with the explanation of human behavior is the foundation from which virtually all interpretive projects commence. What is typically missing, though, is a concern for identifying systematic relationships among the explanatory principles. Consequently, these principles inevitably seem largely superficial, if not ad hoc. The crucial point is that even if they are true, the interest of such principles is limited because they lack depth.

Scientific explanation is, no doubt, continuous with everyday explanation, but it surely falls within the more rigorous region of that continuum (certainly, if science supplies, as most would insist, more determinate knowledge). This continuity between scientific explanation and everyday explanation tempts many to obscure the distinction between the two. The dependence of interpretation upon the principles of everyday explanation tempts many to obscure the distinction between these two too. We strongly suspect that it is these two gaffes that open the door to hermeneutic exclusivism (which, we trust, it is obvious that we reject). Since that position minimizes the differences between the two enterprises, they become functionally interchangeable and the choice between them becomes largely a matter of taste. As a consequence we lose our grip on a vast range of pressing epistemological issues, one of the most important of which is ascertaining those features of our inquiries which lead us to regard them as scientific.

All distinctions (except, perhaps, some of those in logic) fall on some continuum or other, and it is in virtue of this that a little philosophical analysis can always offer grounds for obscuring them. Indeed, this is a worthy basis for distinguishing between two styles of doing philosophy. One emphasizes the continuity of concepts in order to obscure the distinctions between them. The other, by contrast, emphasizes the continuity of concepts in order to improve the distinctions between them, we assume that the contents of this paragraph make it clear into which camp we fall.

We distinguish between science and other knowledge-seeking activities (and between scientific explanation and other types of explanation) for perfectly good reasons' concerning, among other things, maintaining clarity in epistemological inquiry. One of the most important of those reasons, which we will not defend here, is that it is the emergence of modern science that is the preeminent datum of the past millennium for epistemology. The epistemological preeminence of science rests not in its ability to capture the ultimate causal structure of reality (whatever that might mean) but rather in its ability to provide systematic explanations of phenomena that enable us to tackle the problems that we face. (Ironically, it is by theorizing about abstract worlds removed from the world that is the object of our interpretations that we develop the most effective tools for coping with that world of everyday experience.)

Clearly, we wish to defend making these distinctions, but again we take a less restrictive approach than that of the logical empiricists. The problem with the logical empiricists' view was that they distinguished both science and its explanations too narrowly. While the logical empiricists were correct to focus on explanation *in science*, their D-N model of explanation does not exhaust our insights about causal relations or any other available means for explicating systematic empirical relations among phenomena. What are uncontroversially regarded as sciences (and their forms of explanation) have proved far more diverse and freewheeling than logical empiricism and its D-N model ever permitted. Both are unduly confining, as we have indicated above.

By contrast we maintain, in the face of the actual diversity of science, that explanations are more likely to count as scientific to the extent (1) that they operate by means of *systematically related, general principles* that employ concepts at levels of abstraction removed from that by which the phenomena to be explained is currently characterized and (2) that such systems of principles from which explanations proceed are empirically culpable beyond their initial domain of application. This is to say that the clearest cases of scientific explanations are those which stem from independently testable theories. In short, paradigmatic scientific explanation is *theoretical* explanation. In the next few paragraphs, we will comment on this portrait of scientific explanation.

Our account indicates that scientific explanations use principles that are *general*. This concerns the quantity of the propositions in question. A term is general if it refers to a class of entities that has more than one member. A principle is general in one sense if it refers to more than one member of a class of entities that has more than one member. It is general in a stronger sense if it refers to *all* of the members of a class of entities that has more than one member, that is, if it is a universally quantified statement about a class with multiple members. The more general an explanation's principles are the more likely it is, ceteris paribus, to count as scientific.[1]

The least controversially scientific explanations issue from systems of related principles. Science is concerned with how the world (in all of its specificity) hangs together. Consequently, these explanatory systems in science liberate us from the isolation that characterizes so many of the explanations of common sense. In science that sort of isolation is a vice. Unconnected, explanatory principles can only summarize available knowledge, they *cannot* extend it.

By contrast, a *theory* using *abstract* concepts can extend our knowledge. The theoretical systems from which science's explanations follow involve levels of abstraction higher than those that are readily available given existing conceptual schemes—including those of science. Since a theory's various explanatory principles share many of its abstract concepts, no particular explanatory principle fixes a concept's sense or reference. For this reason scientific explanations, unlike those which emerge from common sense, are not conceptually flat. Nor are they conceptually stagnant. In the course of continuing research, a successful theoretical proposal inevitably provokes new explanatory problems, which arise from recognizing that its conceptual resources for the description of a phenomenon are deficient in some important respect. Of course, these explanatory problems provoke new explanatory proposals in their turn. It is the combination of this semantic slack and these sorts of vicissitudes and consequences of a theory's empirical application that motivates the theoretical adjustments that contribute to the growth of knowledge. It is the generality of a theory's explanatory principles, then, in conjunction with the abstractness of its concepts (that those principles mutually employ) that insures that the theory will meet the second requirement that it prove *empirically tractable* in domains beyond that to which it was initially applied. It must extend beyond the domain to which it was initially applied because if the theory pertained only to the principal domain that it was forged to explain, it could be tailor-made in an ad hoc fashion.

It should be reasonably clear by now why the first condition in this account of scientific explanation was temporally qualified as well. It is trivial that the level of abstraction "by which the phenomena to be explained is currently characterized" cannot be that which the newly proposed, explanatory theory uses. Successfully accounting for the pertinent phenomena in terms of the explanatory principles of a new theory which utilizes concepts of greater abstraction will mark explanatory progress. This additional abstraction permits the new theory to group the phenomena in question systematically with other phenomena to which the extant framework had failed to connect it for the purposes of explanation.

Unlike the D-N model of the logical empiricists, this approach to explanation envisions multiple forms of explanation in science. In addition to covering law explanations, scientists develop statistical, functional, and structural explanations as well. All of these types of explanation are heuristics for increasing our systematic knowledge of an empirical domain. For example, McMullin (1978) argues that if a science has developed D-N explanations, then scientists in that field search for a structural account of the mechanisms which realize the relations that the causal laws spotlight. We have argued elsewhere that functional explanation is a valuable strategy for unpacking complex causal relations and for rendering them susceptible to mathematical modeling and nomological analysis (McCauley and Lawson 1984). It is the search for explanations of the forms that are *not* already available in a science which is often the impetus for important leaps in the progress of research. (Consider the effect of Watson's and Crick's formulation of the double helix model of DNA on the development of molecular genetics.) The quest for deeper and more comprehensive explanation in science is an unending process. *Explanation is never ultimate* (Popper 1963). Where ultimate explanation begins science ceases.

If this approach to explanation is correct, then interpretive endeavors penetrate this process at every turn. Exclusivism forces us into making an unnecessary choice between these two types of cognitive pursuits; and inclusivism overemphasizes one at the expense of the other. Both the dichotomies of the exclusivists and the compromises of the inclusivists each fail to recognize the complex and positive relationships that explanation and interpretation have to one another. In the world in which our knowledge grows they interact with each other in quite specific ways. Novel *interpretations* utilize the categories of theories and models already in place. Novel *explanations* require the discovery of new theories and models. On the one hand, as Makkreel shows, the production of new meanings facilitates the generation of new explanatory theories. On the other, as we show, prior explanatory discoveries inform all good interpretation.

When we seek better interpretations, we *assume* the categories of the theories and models at our disposal (Murphy and Medin 1985; Lakoff 1987). When we develop better explanations we might very well start off with a set of established categories, but we might have to abandon them in light of the unexpected implications new models suggest. Interpretations make sense of new experiences on the basis of ready-made conceptual schemes. There is always some view of things already in place. Children are born into a world in which a system of concepts is already at work; the child's job is to discover that system of concepts and to learn how to use it. It is equally true, for child or adult, that no system of concepts suffices for all situations, meets all interests, or serves all purposes.

When people seek better interpretations, they attempt to employ the categories they have in better ways. By contrast, when people seek better explanations, they go beyond the rearrangement of categories; they *generate* new theories which will, if successful, replace or even eliminate the conceptual scheme with which they presently operate (McCauley 1986a).

The growth of knowledge is most profound when a better interpretation in terms of existing categories is not enough (because the extant categories simply cannot do the job). In that case, it is not just that proposed interpretations do not stand the tests of life-experience and common sense (for that would simply be another way of presupposing the strong distinction between theory and observation). The failure to acknowledge the theoretical character of common sense invests it with an undeserved epistemological preeminence in the assessment of novel views. It generates the illusion that *within* the hermeneutic circle common sense constitutes a kind of "objective" standard of knowledge—responsible for the stability that our background knowledge displays.

The most provocative discoveries arise in response to the world's continued resistance to established conceptual schemes. These situations require theorizing which exceeds current conceptual structures and which suggests new possibilities. Revolutions in thought do occur. In science, at least, progress can lead to the wholesale elimination of theories that were previously entrenched. These eliminations are a function of the radical discontinuity of the new theory and the old and the increased explanatory and problem-solving adequacy of the new proposals. Those features, in turn, are overwhelmingly assessed on the basis of the new theory's ability to undergo and pass empirical tests. Implicit in the D-N model of explanation and in logical empiricism's focus on completed theories generally is a failure to recognize these two moments in the growth of knowledge (Cummins 1983: 137–138).

Unlike explanation, interpretation is not so obviously concerned with matters of falsifiability. As Sperber (1985: 28–29) says:

> Interpretive generalizations do not in any way specify what is empirically possible or impossible. They provide a fragmentary answer to a simple single question: what is epistemologically feasible? Not: How are things? But: What representation can be given of things? Such a statement may be easy or hard to corroborate ... but it is beyond falsification.

Note that it follows from this claim that interpretations usually concern more purely conceptual issues (and conceptual relations in particular) than do explanations. Note that it also follows that explanations usually concern more purely empirical issues (and empirical relations in particular) than do interpretations. (We agree with Quine [1953] that distinctions between empirical and conceptual issues cannot be made once and for all. However, the whole thrust of our constructive argument in this chapter has been to show that in any *particular context of inquiry*, distinguishing empirical and conceptual issues, though still a matter of degree, is not only not impossible, but crucial for an account of the progress of scientific knowledge.) If interpretations are not generally falsifiable as Sperber maintains, then they do not make the kinds of systematic empirical claims in terms of which we have characterized explanation in science. If, typically, they do not make systematic empirical claims, then the function of interpretation is surely different from explanation and it is that very difference that makes it possible for the two to interact (Rappaport 1979: 157–158).

Those who downplay the importance of attempts to distinguish between interpretation and explanation on the basis of their relative empirical tractability wish to emphasize the continuities between our methods of criticizing interpretive and explanatory proposals. However, as we maintained before, merely obscuring distinctions never increases knowledge; the proper goal is to improve upon obscure distinctions by formulating more precise ones (but, then, as Whitehead recommended, remaining ever vigilant in our mistrust of newfound clarity).

Explanation and interpretation, then, are different cognitive tasks. They supplement and support one another in the pursuit of knowledge (Sperber 1985: 10). Specifically, interpretations presuppose (and may reorganize) our systematic, empirical knowledge, whereas successful explanatory theories both winnow and increase it. Interpretations uncover unexpected connections in the knowledge we already possess; the success of new explanatory theories establishes new vistas. Consequently, the process of explanation is productive as well. Knowledge is always in the making.

The processes of interpretation and explanation are interrelated and necessary steps in understanding the world and our place in it. If new explanations supplement, modify, or replace existing conceptual schemes, interpretive endeavors reorganize them in order to prepare the ground for further explanation. This interaction is an unending affair.

Our purpose in this chapter has been both to distinguish these two enterprises and to show how they are related. After all, holy matrimony can only join together what were two distinct entities before. We admit the mutual codependence of the two activities; however, we refuse to collapse the distinction. (Husband and wife still remain male and female.) Unlike the inclusivists, we refuse to subordinate one to the other. (Sexism is a sin.) Unlike the exclusivist, we recognize the value of both pursuits. (Attempting to maintain the appearance of self-sufficiency yields a lonely life.)

Our interest in exploring the distinction between interpretation and explanation here is not primarily for its own sake, but rather to investigate their interaction in the growth of knowledge and their interdependence as cognitive activities.

3

Crisis of Conscience, Riddle of Identity: Making Space for a Cognitive Approach to Religious Phenomena

with E. Thomas Lawson

Introduction

Two disciplines are in trouble. For anthropology, this is a relatively new state of affairs. For the history of religions, on the other hand, this has been a persistent condition. Anthropology suffers from a crisis of conscience, the history of religions from a crisis of identity. We shall maintain

(1) that behind both of these crises lurk important epistemological problems,

(2) that historians of religion and many anthropologists have adopted strategies in addressing their crisis of identity that lead to truncated views of religious phenomena,

(3) that a less restricted view of religious phenomena will suggest an approach in the study of religion which neither anthropologists nor historians of religion have adequately explored, and

(4) that the approach in question will go some way toward addressing both the crisis of conscience in anthropology and the riddle of identity in the history of religions.

Section II, "Anthropology and Its Crisis of Conscience," explores the response of anthropology to its history of complicity with colonialist oppression. While we concur with the values that inform many anthropologists' concerns with the ethical consequences of their inquiries, we suggest that the prevailing hermeneutic responses are methodologically ill-advised. They grossly underestimate the promise of analyses of cultural systems that employ systems of general principles that are empirically testable. Since systematicity, generality, and testability are, all things being equal, to be preferred, these oversights have serious epistemological ramifications.

The section "Signs of Religion in the Science of Religion" considers the perennial problem that the history of religions faces concerning its place among the disciplines. Historians of religion typically make three claims about their projects. First, they hold that the history of religions is a specialized discipline focusing on one particular area of human activity and experience. Second, anxious to distinguish themselves from theologians on the one hand and social scientists on the other, historians of religion have also usually located their enterprise among the humanities. Finally, encouraged by both the phenomenological and hermeneutic movements, historians of religion have frequently claimed a special status for either their methods of study, their objects of study, or both. By contrast, we shall maintain both that these three claims are each problematic and that, as practiced, the history of religions has yet to fully free itself from theological assumptions.

Rarely have scholars attacked hermeneutics for its moral failings. Champions of science do not usually appeal to *its* moral virtues. In the sections "The Harmful Effects of the Hermeneutic Method" and "Beyond Guilt" we will do both. The section "The Harmful Effects of the Hermeneutic Method" examines the implications of the hermeneutic emphasis on texts and traditions in the history of religions. We argue that that emphasis offers an incomplete picture of religious phenomena that encourages just the sorts of oversights to which many current anthropologists have reacted. This hermeneutic approach offers little insight into a tremendous range of religious activities, including religious ritual. Nor does it confront the system of knowledge (much of which may be unconscious) that participants in religious systems share. In order to avoid the chauvinism that inevitably accompanies this textual approach and to address those areas of religious phenomena that it tends to ignore (whether in anthropology or the history of religions), we suggest in the section "Beyond Guilt" that researchers in the study of religion look to the cognitive sciences for inspiration.

Anthropology and its crisis of conscience

It is by now no secret that anthropology—in its role as the science of culture—inadvertently provided much of the intelligence that contributed to the oppression of the peoples it studied. As a consequence, many anthropologists are abandoning explanatory theorizing and some are abandoning science altogether out of guilt about the role that anthropological research has played in colonial repression, for example, by providing information to governmental agencies about the people they were studying and by suggesting means for their control.

These anthropologists hold the view that the moral insensitivity inherent in these developments is finally grounded in a kind of cultural insensitivity that is the inevitable result of intrusive scientific concerns with prediction and control. They not only wish to resurrect the traditional distinction between the natural and the cultural (between things and people, between the *Naturwissenschaften* and the *Geisteswissenschaften*), they then wish to deny the possibility of a human science that operates along the lines of the natural sciences. Their moral sensitivities demand that people be treated differently from things. Because of their moral concerns (which we applaud) these anthropologists advocate the adoption of a new, non-manipulative hermeneutic model for anthropological research. On this model, anthropology looks to the humanities and their characteristic concern with the interpretation and understanding (in contrast to the explanation and control) of cultural materials. The new agenda of this "romantic rebellion" (Shweder 1984) mandates the interpretation rather than the explanation of cultures and cultures' texts (Geertz 1973; Clifford and Marcus 1986).

While hermeneutic approaches to cultural materials may salve anthropologists' consciences, they may well do so at the price of generating problems of comparable gravity concerning the epistemic status of this sort of anthropological research (Sperber 1985). This hermeneutic turn has led these anthropologists to throw the scientific baby out with the colonialist bath water, much to the distress of those anthropologists who have continued to pursue a scientific agenda (Sperber 1985; O'Meara 1989; Boyer 1990). Appropriately anticolonialist, hermeneutically oriented anthropologists are also, sadly, antitheoretical—thereby forfeiting the opportunity to increase our systematic knowledge of cultural forms. The fact of the matter is that only novel explanatory theorizing can break through the confines of the hermeneutic circle (Lawson and McCauley 1990).

This precipitous methodological response to moral concerns has provoked in cultural anthropology a predicament. How can anthropology lay claim to scientific respectability while overthrowing the very considerations that make sciences scientific? The irony in all of this is that after decades of trying to establish their scientific respectability (White 1949; Spiro 1966; Horton 1967; Jarvie 1972; Kaplan and Manners 1972), many cultural anthropologists now face their colleagues' capitulation to antiscientific hysteria and their relinquishing of their scientific aspirations to the *biological* anthropologists. In short, this strategy for reconceiving cultural anthropology as humanistic inquiry in the hermeneutic mode may buy sensitivity and moral rectitude but at the cost of forfeiting its place among the sciences. What is missing is the recognition that the connection between scientific aspirations for anthropological research and collusion with imperialism is not a necessary one. Certainly, the two issues are logically independent.

The proper course is not for cultural anthropologists to abandon explanatory theorizing in favor of either hermeneutic circling, idiographic research, or even detailed ethnography, but rather for them to take a more active role in influencing the disposition and use of the knowledge they produce. Producers who disseminate their products, whether conceptual or material, can never completely control the use of those products. Nor can we expect them to. If they seriously examine the moral implications of their labors and their labors' products, and they act in good faith to promote their proper and constructive use, then such producers are not automatically culpable morally. These cultural anthropologists correctly maintain that anthropological scientists and scientists in general have far too often failed to recognize these responsibilities, but it hardly follows that the optimal response in the face of such failures is to forsake science!

Of course, most hermeneutically oriented anthropologists are not especially unhappy about "putting science in its place." They feel justified by some recent research in the history, philosophy, and sociology of science that suggests that science has never deserved its special epistemic status in any case (Bloor 1981: 199–213). Positivism is dead. Scientific practice often contradicts philosophical pronouncements about the nature of science. The distinctions between the normative and the descriptive and between theory and observation are almost impossible to sustain, and the sociocultural and historical context in which scientific activity takes place influences scientists' agendas in fundamental ways. In sum, these anthropologists have become convinced that science faces just as many epistemic tangles as any other knowledge-seeking activity. So why, they ask, should science be accorded preeminent epistemic standing? If these portraits of science have any verisimilitude, then little is lost in anthropology abandoning scientific pretensions. Still, such portraits of science are not uncontroversial. Suffice it to say, we are unsympathetic with the view that nonrational influences on the process of scientific research somehow undermine its rational character (see Thagard 1992).

The romantic rebellion in anthropology has drawn considerable encouragement from recent trends in Continental thought. Various schools of thought (deconstructionism most prominently) have not only sounded anticolonialist themes and emphasized the epistemic binds in which all contenders for knowledge find themselves but they have also highlighted the connections between these two phenomena. These schools stress the social forces that constrain the construction of knowledge and, more broadly, the central role that contextual considerations play in that process. They underscore the ties between the power of knowledge and the treatment of human beings.

By contrast, we maintain that distinctions of relative epistemic honor are valuably made and not so easy to sweep under the rug—no matter what the winds of fashion deposit on our intellectual doorsteps. What counts as knowledge, how it is obtained, and how it is certified are problems that just will not go away, at least so long as knowledge claims conflict. Conflicting knowledge claims require attention because questions of authority, truth, reliability, utility, and value arise no matter what the epistemological framework. The anthropologist who wishes to interpret rather than explain culture still faces the problem of adjudicating between *different* interpretations. Even if "anything goes" not everything arrives! One of the major goals of philosophical inquiry is to examine such conflicts. After all, in situations of conflict which knowledge-seeking activities are to be deferred to? Whose word can be taken? What can we depend upon? What is most useful in this situation? What is more important here? Forging satisfactory answers to such questions is not abetted by lumping all of our knowledge claims together for monolithic treatment. For whatever reasons, human beings do supply answers in such situations. If some of those answers prove demonstrably superior to others as descriptions of the world (or as solutions to the problems at hand), then it is perfectly reasonable to wonder if general principles underlie the strategies that generated those superior responses. Epistemology will never go away.

Few, if any, of the recent skeptics about science have completely denied the relatively greater determinateness and precision of evidential standards in science in comparison to those of other forms of inquiry. Determinateness and precision of evidential standards are virtues worthy of preservation because they show a respect for the subject matter, for the proposals made to account for it, and even for the people making the proposals (McCauley 1992). The failure to recognize these virtues where they occur exacts an unacceptable toll. No disciplines more carefully monitor the integrity of their findings. Many nonscientific disciplines have few explicit standards for even distinguishing the well-founded from what is not. Without such evidential standards, either the directions of disciplines are at the mercy of the whims of the powerful or anything goes. Science does not enjoy sole proprietorship of these (or any other) epistemic virtues. It does, however, most clearly exemplify these virtues on the hoof.

If epistemic virtues collapse, can moral virtues be far behind? What unifies epistemic and moral virtues is the concern for honesty and truth (however it is to be defined). On this front at least, epistemic and moral virtues are cut from the same cloth. With the collapse of epistemic distinctions, what will happen to the moral awareness that kindled the guilt and precipitated anthropology's crisis of conscience in the first place? We shall maintain in the section "The Harmful Effects of the Hermeneutic Method" that anthropology's retreat from its scientific aspirations has both epistemic and moral implications. To atone for recent or even ancient ethnocentric sins is admirable; to abandon effective means of inquiry is self-defeating and hinders the growth of knowledge. Among other things, scientific endeavors can offer insights about why we committed such sins in the first place.

Signs of religion in the science of religion: The history of religions and the riddle of its identity

In the midst of the well-publicized crisis in anthropology, many have missed a closely related predicament in another field which is also involved with the analysis of particular cultural forms. Many of anthropology's interests intersect with and are further developed in the history of religions (also sometimes referred to as "comparative religion" or "Religionswissenschaft"). The situation here, however, is even graver than that of anthropology. Not only does it frequently rely upon the results of anthropological research (immediately calling into question some historians' of religions claims to autonomy for their field and, in the bargain, forcing them to confront the epistemic crisis that cultural anthropology faces), but, in addition, the history of religions must also clarify its position among the disciplines. It faces more than a crisis of conscience; it must also solve the riddle of its identity. It is to that topic that we now turn.

Any perusal of their frequent methodological ruminations will disclose that historians of religions in both Europe and North America have never been comfortable about being associated, on the one hand, with the social sciences or, on the other, with theology.[1] Historians of religion have always been suspicious of theology

(1) because of its obvious religious assumptions,
(2) because of its bias toward those categories developed in Western religions in general and in Christianity in particular,
(3) because of its explicative function within the conceptual scheme of particular religious traditions,
(4) because of its role in religious apologetics (defending the faith against hostile cultural criticism), and
(5) because of its normative (rather than descriptive) focus.

While historians of religions were (and still often continue to be) housed in theological faculties or divinity schools in Europe and North America, the rapid expansion of departments of religion in public universities in the 1960s in North America and England, and the establishment of some chairs in Religionswissenschaft outside of theological faculties in Europe, permitted their relocation in either the humanities or in area or interdisciplinary programs of one kind or another. These moves reinforced opportunities for systematic, focused research on religion largely independent of religious institutions and their inevitable theological concerns. They also bolstered the impression that a new discipline was in good working order which was free from theological taint.

This new breed, safely removed from theological faculties, has not only been suspicious of theology, it has also been distrustful of its new academic neighbors, especially those housed in the social sciences. One of the early historians of religion, Joachim Wach, argued very forcefully that the history of religions was neither a social science nor a theological discipline (Wach 1988a, b). He did, however, insist upon maintaining a dialogue with theologians and was responsible for moving "comparative religion" out of the humanities division and into the Divinity School of the University of Chicago.

Recently, Wendy Doniger (1988: 21) has continued Wach's refrain:

> Historians of religions must fight a war on two fronts. The first battle is against the covert truth claims of theological approaches to religion that masquerade as non-theological approaches…. But the historian of religions must also be on guard against the overt objections of superrationalists, who oppose the study of religion in *any* form or would allow it to be studied only within the sterile confines of an objectivity that is in any case impossible and probably not even desirable. It is a razor's edge not at all easy to tread, but it is the Middle Way for the humanistic study of religion.

This comment contains much with which we agree. The history of religions *should* resist theology at all costs. We also side with Doniger in suspecting that positivist social science is not likely to provide many penetrating insights about religion, and we certainly concur with her resistance to those who oppose the study of religion in any form. Finally, we too propose what we take to be a middle way. However, we cannot fail to note that Doniger has not made a case for establishing a separate discipline of the history of religions *within the humanities*![2]

Why must that middle way traverse humanistic terrain? Why not instead consider a reformed social science (intimately informed by the post-positivistic developments in the history and philosophy of science) or, better yet (we will argue), a new cognitive science of religious *systems*? Before sketching a case for the latter possibility in the final section, we turn, first, to consider the long-standing attempt of the history of religions to edge its way into the humanities.

Perhaps, given its name, the history of religions is a subdiscipline within history. Two considerations suggest that this will not satisfy its practitioners.

First, most historians of religion openly acknowledge that history is a subsidiary and not a central concern. They wish to do focused research on religious texts and institutions, and much of their research seeks conclusions that are both synchronic and (therefore) general. Second, if the history of religions is but a subfield of history, then historians of religions would have no basis for insisting either on the separate, autonomous status of their pursuits (there is, after all, no discrete, independent discipline of the history of law) or on the privileged perspective of their enterprise, their claims for which we shall criticize below straightaway.

The standard line in defense of these claims for the autonomy of the history of religions among the humanities is to argue that it possesses a unique object of study, a unique method for studying that object, or both (Pye 1982). We are unsympathetic with these sorts of claims. The first problem is that the rationales that historians of religion offer in defense of the distinctiveness of their objects of study seem to inevitably involve covert theological assumptions.

Rudolf Otto's *The Idea of the Holy* had a profound influence on the development of the history of religions (Penner 1989). Otto contended that religious experience was *sui generis,* involving "an original and underivable capacity of the mind implanted in 'pure reason' independently of all perception" (Otto 1958: 112). The obvious question concerns what evidence Otto could offer for this claim, especially in light of the fact that numerous individuals disavow any religious impulses whatsoever.

Otto wavered about whether the faculties and capacities in question were principally cognitive or affective; however, he was quite explicit about the special sensitivities necessary for successful study of religious phenomena:

> The reader is invited to direct his mind to a moment of deeply-felt religious experience, as little as possible qualified by other forms of consciousness. Whoever cannot do this, whoever knows no such moments in his experience, is requested to read no farther; for it is not easy to discuss questions of religious psychology with one who can recollect the emotions of his adolescence, the discomforts of indigestion, or say, social feelings, but cannot recall any intrinsically religious feelings. (1958: 8)

It is not clear how talk of "intrinsically religious feelings" that are not "social feelings" (or feelings of some other ordinary sort) can be anything other than thoroughly theological. What motivation is there for claiming that religious feelings are both *sui generis* and irreducible absent a theological agenda?[3]

Further evidence of the theological character of historians' of religions claims for the distinctiveness of their objects of study lies in their characteristic use of concepts pregnant with the aura of transcendence such as "the sacred" and "the Holy" (Preus 1987). Historians of religions rarely seem to feel much need to explicate these kinds of covertly theological terms that so regularly populate their claims. In fact, when they do attempt to explicate such terms, their discussions regularly involve either unacceptably small circles, explicit theological assumptions, or both. Eliade's (1961: 10–11) discussion of "the sacred" displays both flaws: "The first possible definition of the *sacred* is that it is the *opposite of the profane* .... Man becomes aware of the sacred because it manifests itself, shows itself, as something wholly different from the profane." Eliade uses but two terms ("sacred" and "profane"), which are completely inter-defined on the basis of their putative opposition. The opposition establishes an unbridgeable, theologically grounded gulf between the two. Its ground is theological, because Eliade attributes powers, manifestations, agency, and transcendence (of the world of everyday affairs, that is, transcendence of the profane) to the sacred.

While all definitions are circular, all things considered, large circles are preferable to small ones. Eliade's circle is the smallest circle possible! If it does not serve to initiate fruitful theorizing and extend the range of available conceptual connections, then the circularity in question grows more vicious by the minute. In fact, Eliade's principal use of these definitions is merely to illustrate them, repeatedly—cosmos and history, birth and rebirth, and so on. Eliade's covert theological maneuvers are not much different from explicit theological activity *within* contemporary Western religious communities.

Despite their best intentions, then, considerable evidence indicates that historians of religion reimport theological assumptions in the course of making their case for the special status of their inquiry. Furthermore, the humanities offer little precedent (beyond the claims of phenomenologists) for claims either about unique methods or unique objects of study. So, if their standard case for the uniqueness of their endeavors works, then (at best) the history of religions is quite unlike any of the other humanities.

The story does not end here, though. Not all appeals in the history of religions for special objects and methods are so clearly theological. Some historians of religions seem to have other sources of methodological inspiration. Two such sources are phenomenology and hermeneutics. Phenomenologists hold that there is something special about the subject's (in this case, religious) experience that scientific categories and principles cannot capture (Penner 1989: 41–61). Hermeneutics involves the view that interpretive approaches give us the best (and perhaps only) understanding of cultural systems such as religion. We shall discuss the issue of subjectivity first and then turn to the question of interpretation.

Phenomenologists maintain that human subjectivity transcends our ordinary modes of description and, consequently, evades any explanatory net (Penner 1989: 47). The category of "subjectivity" on this view is of a different order than the categories for things. Subjectivity is "grasped" or "intuited" in its various "manifestations." Historians of religions enlist these phenomenological claims in behalf of the special, nonobjective status of human subjectivity in order to defend their claims for the special character of religious experience (Bleeker 1975).

Especially attractive to those historians of religion wary of appearing to endorse the truth of particular religious claims is the phenomenologists' technique of "bracketing" experience. Since phenomenology is concerned with the architecture of consciousness, it does not concern itself with questions about the truth-values of our claims. It is simply concerned with the development of neutral categories for assessing the form of presentation of the world in our subjective life. It is concerned with the world only as it is subjectively apprehended, not with the world as it is in itself. The descriptions that result from the bracketing of (claims about) our experience in this sense are alleged to be unbiased and decontextualized. They only capture the world the way consciousness apprehends it.

The resources of phenomenology enable historians of religion to distance themselves from theology on at least two fronts. First, bracketing religious experience eliminates the need to assess the truth-values of the resulting religious claims (Wach 1988a: 22). The historian of religion, *qua* phenomenologist, is concerned solely with the subjective character of religious experience. Bracketing religious experience permits the historian of religion to suspend judgment about the putative objects of those religious states. Second, phenomenologists, like historians of religions, contend that they are engaged in a purely descriptive endeavor. So construed, the history of religions avoids any traces of the nonnative character of theology. In sum, then, phenomenology encourages the impression that historians of religions can find refuge in the humanities, supports their conviction that scientific categories do not apply to their special subject matter and suggests that they can have this all without succumbing to theology.

Let us concede for the moment both that the concepts of "consciousness" and "subjectivity" are used univocally and coherently throughout phenomenological discussions and that such a phenomenological approach represents a genuine attempt to provide an alternative to scientific accounts of important and even mysterious features of selves-in-the-world. Still, in the face of research in the cognitive and neuro-sciences concerning such phenomena as implicit knowledge, priming, belief perseverance, and attribution and in the area of neural pathology concerning various functional deficits and the accompanying confabulation, phenomenologists' contentions that the forms of conscious experience and subjectivity elude explanatory analysis are not particularly compelling (Nisbett and Ross 1980; Churchland 1986; Stich 1990). At most, the phenomenological ploy enables historians of religions to raise questions about the allegations of the *scientistically inclined* concerning the eventual exhaustiveness of such explanatory endeavors.

The claims of many prominent historians of religions who willingly characterize themselves as phenomenologists (such as Van Der Leeuw 1963) concerning the special status of their inquiries seem frequently to be religiously motivated through and through. As Preus has shown, such motivations have their roots in the development of the study of religion in the West. Preus (1987) argues that the study of religion started with the *criticism* of religion from *within* (the Christian) religion. At first that meant criticism of religions *other* than Christianity, which remained privileged and exempt. Such criticism provided "theological explanations" of other cultures' religious practices. Eventually, though, such criticism inspired psychological and sociological explanations that were applicable to *all* religious forms (including those of Christianity) and that were independent of religious institutions. This secularization of explanations of religious phenomena found full flower in the work of such figures as Durkheim and Freud.

According to Preus' account, historians of religion represent a special tradition of scholarship. While acknowledging the importance of criticizing religion, and while recognizing the need to cease exempting Christianity from critical analysis, and even while conceding the importance of abandoning a theological perspective, historians of religions never took the final step of completely purging their positions of theological claims. Although historians of religions sought refuge from theology in order to avoid privileging any *one* form of religious subjectivity, *what they failed to recognize was that they were still attempting to privilege religious subjectivity generally.* That was consonant with a peculiarly modern form of theology that emphasized the universality of theological categories for making sense of religious experience as such (in terms of such notions as "ultimate concern," the "feeling of absolute dependence," etc.). Paul Tillich even talked about a theology of the history of religions (Tillich 1963)!

Historians of religion have repeatedly come remarkably close to freeing themselves from theology. What has prevented their final liberation, though, has not so much been their willingness to adopt phenomenologists' assumptions but rather their attempt to adapt them in the service of their field's traditional claims concerning the special status of religious experience (Long 1986). They have never abandoned the attempt to make a case for a special kernel of religious subjectivity that would remain forever insulated from scientific analyses. Instead, they have continued to presume that making a case for their special subject matter would suffice to establish both the uniqueness and autonomy of their pursuits and protect religion from reductionistic programs in the natural and social sciences. As a simple matter of fact, the history of religions has never been able to wean itself fully from the succor provided by assumptions that are, ultimately, theological (Pals 1986, 1990).

Hermeneutics has provided a second source of inspiration for those historians of religion seeking a safe haven in the humanities. Historically, of course, hermeneutics had its origins both in the interpretation of biblical texts and in the apologetics of those theologians, such as Schleiermacher, who were grasping for new ways to defend Western religion, and especially Christianity, in its hour of travail in the aftermath of the Enlightenment. That cultural movement which had precipitated the internal criticism of religion had had powerful effects. Theologians were not about to let the ship of religion sink without radical rescue maneuvers. Schleiermacher's hermeneutics, rather than being anti-theological, then, explicitly functioned as an *apologia* for religion by attempting to provide a special experiential grounding (the feeling of absolute dependence) for both the religious life and theology of his time, a theology whose conceptual basis and significance was under attack.

Contemporary hermeneutics, of course, has moved away from its early theological roots. It no longer presupposes explicitly religious metaphors and concerns in its disquisitions. It has provided historians of religions with a new guiding metaphor, namely, "The Text," which has attracted historians of religion searching for non-theological support for their convictions about the immunity of features of religious experience from scientific analysis.

Those cultural anthropologists who have abandoned explanatory theorizing in favor of hermeneutic explorations have only heartened historians of religions on this count. Historians of religions have jumped at the chance to enlist hermeneutically aligned cultural anthropologists. They are grateful for allies with a "humanistic" rather than a "theological" or "scientific" orientation (Segal 1989). This hermeneutic approach permits historians of religion not only to interpret religious texts but to interpret religion as a whole *as a textual object*. By focusing on the interpretation rather than the explanation of religious phenomena, historians of religions intend not only to resist "scientism" (a worthy act, indeed!) but, unfortunately (by our lights), to oppose science as well (hence, Doniger's pronouncements about the "sterile confines of an objectivity that is … impossible and probably not even desirable").

The harmful effects of the hermeneutic method

Proposals to situate the study of religion among the humanities that are grounded in the adoption of a hermeneutic approach severely truncate inquiry about religion (Geertz 1973; Clifford and Marcus 1986). That approach appeals to the particular over the general. It is unconcerned with systematic patterns. It is usually historicist in the extreme. Most important, though, it privileges in the study of religion not only religious texts but the category of textuality in general.

The problem, in short, is that religious systems are not texts. The hermeneutic method must be force-fitted to those features of religious systems (or any symbolic-cultural system) which are not literary. Obvious examples include ritual, a wide array of non-ritual religious practices, and nearly all iconography. The insistence on construing all cultural phenomena along textual lines inevitably blinds inquirers to many of their nonlinguistic features.

This comment may seem incompatible with the position we advance in *Rethinking Religion*. It is not. Here we are attacking an analogy between religion and texts. There we employ an analogy between the underlying *structures* of religious systems and the *grammars* of natural languages. There is no contradiction. Although texts always arise within some natural language, neither natural languages nor their underlying grammatical structures are texts. The concept of a "natural language" presupposes neither the concept of "literacy" nor the concept of a "text." Plenty of natural languages have existed in which no speaker-listeners have *ever* produced a text!

The most pernicious implication of adopting the hermeneutic method as the exclusive approach to the study of religion follows from this inability of the textual analogy to address the wide range of religious activities, objects, and practices that do not fit the textual mold (whether because the phenomena in question are actions or because they originate in nonliterate societies or because they employ non-propositional forms of representation). The textual straightjacket that hermeneutic methods impose leaves many features of symbolic-cultural systems (not just religious systems) in a cognitive vacuum. It discourages serious consideration of, among other things, the vast majority of religious actions of the vast majority of religious people. This hermeneutic approach especially encourages the neglect of religious practices in nonliterate societies.

Another implication of the textual model employed by the hermeneutically inclined scholar is its emphasis upon a self-conscious sense of history. This is of a piece with the textual focus insofar as "history" (in the scholar's sense of the term) is textually based. Focusing upon history generates a tendency to overvalue the recording of traditions and textual memory and, therefore, tends to generate a dismissive attitude toward all those people of the world whose cultures are not organized along such lines. This plays directly into colonialists' hands, since they have standardly justified their cultural imperialism on the basis of their claim that "the primitives" had no traditions (because they had no texts).

A notion of "tradition" exists, however, that is basically independent of such a self-conscious sense of history grounded in texts (Boyer 1990). The notion in question focuses on "traditions" as cultural habits and customs (for which participants may have no knowledge whatsoever of those practices' historical roots). It is in this sense of "tradition" that nonliterate peoples of the world have frequently had *their* traditions stripped away by the forces of colonialism. At least implicitly, both historians of religions and cultural anthropologists have always recognized this sense of the term "tradition." After all, it is, presumably, with this notion of "tradition" in mind that they have so frequently labeled nonliterate cultures "traditional."

It is also this sense of "tradition" that hermeneutically inspired inquiries largely ignore. Not only are the practices not texts, the culture often does not even possess texts that describe them. About such cultures and about their religious practices in particular, then, hermeneutically oriented approaches have very little to say—*even though the peoples in question have rich and interesting religious lives and religious systems* that are both creative and complex. (Crucially, the types of phenomena in question have been the stock and trade of the traditional, scientific approaches in anthropology! Why should these nonliterary cultural achievements be excluded from serious scholarly analysis?)

Further, a hermeneutical approach far too easily leads to a taxonomic strategy that labels a vast sea of human beings as "primitive" in contrast to the civilized few. Once so identified, these peoples can once again be viewed as a different type of human being, lower on the evolutionary scale, incapable of sustaining serious thought, deficient in high culture, and worthy of patronizing treatment and subjugation. Herein lie the roots of cultural chauvinism and racism and most of the other moral failings that so concerned the anthropologists we discussed at the outset of this paper.

Such emphases upon texts and traditions have consequences in common. The first of these is the insulation of Christianity and the so-called World Religions. It has always been clear, though seldom acknowledged, that an understanding of religion that limits the subject matter either to texts or textually based traditions favors some religious systems at the expense of others. In an earlier era, dominated by a colonialist and imperialist mentality, such a strategy might have seemed acceptable, but in the "global village" such narrow-mindedness is not only out of place but execrable. We must talk about *all* religious phenomena when we study religion, not just those that arise within the framework of long-standing textually based traditions possessing massive literary resources.

The second consequence of the double emphasis upon text and tradition involves establishing (in the style of Eliade) additional unilluminating, ethnocentric dichotomies—for example, between low and high, established and popular, folk and elite—which then license a kind of discourse about people that is destructive of human community. Obviously, these dichotomies, which both historians of religions and anthropologists regularly employ, embody valuations. These scholars compare practices and concepts from each side of these dichotomies and conclude what they have already assumed, namely, that the characteristics of "the higher" are more complex, more sophisticated, and consequently more significant than those of "the lower." So, for example, it is the thought and behavior of only some of the people in any culture that merit full-fledged interpretative consideration. The irony in all of this is that, whereas insensitivity is not supposed to be a mark of civilization, from the very bowels of high culture emerges the grossest sort of insensitivity to the "savages"—who may have a sex life worthy of interest but not a religion by "civilized" standards!

Even if we concede that the principal business of the humanities is the study of texts and traditions, we reject the views which hold that texts and traditions exhaust religious phenomena, that they are the most fundamental features of religion, and that religious systems are not subject to explanatory theorizing. We reject, in effect, the suggestion that the humanities and hermeneutic methods in particular can supply an exhaustive account of what is interesting about religion. Indeed, we are suggesting that the hermeneutic approach misses fundamental features about religious activities as they exist in the vast array of current and previous cultures.

In *Rethinking Religion*, what we take to be most fundamental and common to all religious phenomena is that they occur within a symbolic-cultural system that includes presumptions about superhuman agents (Goody 1961; Spiro 1966). This substantive commitment concerning religion is tantamount to offering a definition. That does not mean that we set great store in arguing endlessly over definitions, since we hold that definitions are driven by and grounded in explanatory theories and are not too interesting apart from their contribution to those theories' explanatory accomplishments. (We should emphasize that this is a comment about the *definitions* of concepts, not the concepts which are defined.) In fact, definitions are only as good as the theories that inspire them. Correspondingly, those theories are only as good as the problem-solving power, explanatory suggestiveness, generality, and empirical testability of their principles. We readily acknowledge that the social sciences have had only limited success in offering productive theories of this sort. This is one of the reasons why so many social scientists have opted for the hermeneutic vortex.[4] By contrast, we hold that this well may be an area where the cognitive sciences can contribute.

Consider, for example, that on a hermeneutic approach, when religions are newborn, they cannot be religions, since they do not yet possess either texts or traditions. And yet what happens subsequently is continuous with what went on before.

Neanderthals almost certainly performed burial practices. These practices are, quite probably, an instance of religious ritual action, involving presumptions about superhuman agents (possibly the deceased themselves) capable of affecting the fact of death in some way or other. Such practices were not repeatedly reinvented each time a member of the community expired. Even if the *material* evidence in such cases is insufficient to justify according these practices the honorific status of a religion, it is inescapable that such cooperative, coordinated, symbolic practices could not have arisen without the participants sharing an extensive body of knowledge. Even if hermeneutically inclined scholars are unwilling to describe these phenomena as constituting "religious systems" in the full-blown sociocultural sense, such practices could not have arisen without the Neanderthal practitioners sharing a *system* of (religious) knowledge. As with the participants in the most elaborate contemporary manifestations of institutionalized religion, these prehistorical participants enjoyed, in common, mastery of a religious system cognitively construed.

Scholars of religion cannot afford to ignore such phenomena. We propose as an alternative to the hermeneutically inspired, textually based notion of "religion" the concept of a religious system as a system of *shared knowledge*, which is cognitively represented in the minds of participants. This system of shared knowledge concerns at least a religious conceptual scheme (which is sometimes discussed in texts and sometimes not and which makes presumptions about culturally postulated superhuman agents) and a system of ritual practices. On this view religion is a phenomenon that predates civilization, history, and textually based traditions. Our principal theoretical object is the knowledge that participants share about both the relevant system of ritual acts and the accompanying conceptual scheme—on the assumption that an account of this shared system of knowledge will go a long way toward explaining many of the behaviors of the participants that it inspires (Lawson and McCauley 1990: 5).

Rethinking religion requires reaffirming the central role of explanatory theorizing in constructing new knowledge about religion. It does not require special privileges.

Beyond guilt: Prospects for a cognitive approach to the study of religious systems

It is time to chart a new path in the study of religion, a path that both anthropology and the history of religions can pursue without moral, epistemic, or methodological qualms.

To begin with the narrowest battle, in a new academic study of religion, the study of religion must genuinely free itself from theology. We have already indicated that we believe that any insistence upon a unique object or method will inevitably founder on theological rocks.

The next question is whether the study of religion should be modeled on the humanities or the sciences. In criticizing phenomenological and hermeneutic approaches in the study of religion, we do not mean to reject interpretive pursuits outright. Instead, our target is *hermeneutic exclusivism*, which tries to insulate certain phenomena from scientific analysis and reserve it for interpretive treatment alone. Over the past few decades a serious imbalance has arisen in the study of religion in favor of such interpretive pursuits. Our goal, in part, is to redress that imbalance (Lawson and McCauley 1990).

We do hold that science is still our premier activity for gaining knowledge about the world. Only science faithfully insures that its principles, from which its various explanations proceed, are, simultaneously, theoretically inspired, systematically related, empirically testable, and general.

Theoretical strategies familiar in the cognitive sciences show special promise for the study of sociocultural systems such as religion (Boyer 1990). In *Rethinking Religion*, we focused on the promise of the competence approach to theorizing in linguistics for theoretical proposals concerning religious ritual systems. Competence theories offer a systematic account of the tacit knowledge of a participant in a symbolic-cultural system. They describe the system of shared knowledge that any participant must have mastered in order to successfully participate in the systems in question. The standard method in linguistic inquiry (which we have adapted in *Rethinking Religion*) is to describe such systems of knowledge by means of a generative system of rules.

Appropriating this strategy for the study of religion suggests a number of interesting analogies between various linguistic and religious phenomena. These analogies are particularly apposite in the case of religious ritual, since both ritual and language appear highly rule-governed. Both speakers of natural languages and participants in religious rituals demonstrate a mastery of a shared body of cultural knowledge that guides and shapes their behavior. In addition, ritual participants easily form a wide array of intuitive judgments about the relative acceptability of the forms of their religious rituals and about those rituals' meanings. This is just like the intuitions of native speaker-listeners that bear on the syntactic and semantic properties of linguistic strings in the language of which they have command.

Like the grammars of natural languages, any system of principles that informs participants' ritual competencies must be both generative and highly structured. Few doubt that religious ritual is highly structured. Whether some system of principles that underlies them must be generative or not is probably less clear. A speaker-listener's abilities to produce and comprehend completely novel linguistic strings is uncontroversial. Participants' creativity with their religious ritual systems is certainly less obvious. After all, to say that the production of new rituals occurs *far* less frequently than does the production of new sentences would (still) be a serious *understatement*. Opportunities for such creativity within religious ritual systems are quite rare (by comparison with our opportunities to produce novel utterances). Still, what we do know is that both new rituals and new religions do arise.

Once we acknowledge the possibility of explanatory theorizing about religion and recognize the suggestiveness of the specific strategies of the cognitive sciences, we have, in fact, proposed a new option to previous styles of theorizing within the social sciences emerging from the work of Durkheim, Freud, and others. We have made room for the study of religion with a theoretical object that resides at the border between the cognitive and the cultural?[5]

We offer a promising approach to the study of religion modeled upon strategies in the cognitive sciences. We think that such an approach brings both predicaments—the crisis of conscience and the riddle of identity—to a satisfactory resolution. The riddle of identity endemic to the history of religions would dissolve if this rootless discipline would plant itself firmly in the soil that nurses all those sciences, social and cognitive, which concern themselves with human thought and action and which recognize the key role that systems of knowledge play in accounting for important aspects of human behavior. Most specifically such a discipline would identify itself as a cognitive science that aims to devise explanatory theories about the forms of knowledge typical of religious systems and the roles such systems of knowledge play in religious action. As a cognitive science, the study of religion will not eschew interpretation but employ it in conjunction with its productive explanatory theories. And even though this newly situated discipline of the study of religion emphasizes the cognitive aspects of religious systems, it will seek to connect such inquiries to the results of research in the related humanities and social sciences.

This approach also promises to diminish, if not dissolve, the crisis of conscience characteristic of interpretive anthropology as well. A cognitive approach to symbolic-cultural materials avoids the pitfalls of a hermeneutic fashion that is constantly waiting to entrap anthropological *litterateurs* who insist on treating the complexities of culture exclusively in textual terms. The cognitive approach (just like any approach in science) plays no favorites. It insists upon seeking principles which are general and, therefore, apply without special privileges to all religious phenomena in all places and at all times. In fact, the cognitive approach finally places the subject matter of the study of religion on the same theoretical footing as any other in the sciences of the human. Such an approach is methodologically sound, theoretically productive, and morally defensible. What more could we expect?

Who Owns 'Culture'?

with E. Thomas Lawson

Introduction

No one owns 'culture'[1]: anyone with a viable theoretical proposal can contend for the right to determine that concept's fate. Not everyone agrees with this view. Throughout its century-long struggle for academic respectability, anthropology has regularly insisted on its *unique* role as the proprietor of 'culture.' Its variety of approaches and feuding factions notwithstanding, it is this proprietary claim that unifies anthropology to an extent sometimes unrecognized even by its own (postmodernist) practitioners. The history of anthropology has witnessed at least three important moments in the case for autonomous cultural phenomena based, first, on traditional ontological and methodological presumptions, second, on the hermeneutic turn, and third, on postmodern analyses of discourses and their influences.

Historically, anthropologists cite two closely related bases for these proprietary presumptions. The first, which we shall not belabor here, hearkens to inevitably vague discussions about culture's autonomy (with various passes at making sense of the *ontological* foundations of that alleged autonomy). Cultural anthropologists have advanced such claims for a century, but Clifford Geertz' gloss on this topic is representative both in what it endorses and in the vagueness of the grounds for the endorsement. While advancing a host of claims about culture's ontological status (e.g., [1] that culture is "ideational," [2]

We wish to thank the American Academy of Religion for their support of this research in the form of an AAR Collaborative Research Grant. We are also grateful to Pascal Boyer, Marshall Gregory, and Charles Nuckolls for helpful comments and encouragement.

that it, nonetheless, "does not exist in someone's head," [3] that it has the same status—whatever *that* is—as a Beethoven quartet, and [4] that it is "public," Geertz insists that "the thing to ask ... is not what ... [its] ontological status is" (Geertz 1973: 10–12). Unfortunately for Geertz and cultural anthropology generally, any convincing case for the autonomy of culture must account for its relations to the things that constitute it. Moreover, because Geertz never relinquishes anthropology's scientific aspirations, the issue of clarifying such ontological questions will persistently arise (McCauley n.d.).[2]

Traditionally, the second basis for anthropologists' alleged ownership of 'culture' concerns the *methodological* consequences of their presumptions about cultural autonomy. Historically, anthropologists have supposed (1) that both cultural wholes and whole cultures exceed the sums of their parts, (2) that culture enjoys a dynamic of its own that could never be reduced to the various decisions of its individual participants, and (3) that the anthropologist's job is to analyze culture's structures and functions in terms of uniquely *cultural* categories.

More recently, whether supplementing or supplanting the historic argument, interpretive anthropologists have emphasized the notion of 'culture' as publicly shared meanings that are not subject to reductive explanation but provide the very framework in which all explanation, indeed, all human endeavor takes its shape. Explicating culture requires understanding, in any particular case, the myriad details that enrich the hermeneutic quest. While this move offers access to 'culture' to anyone with interpretive skills, legitimacy as a cultural commentator also requires a fieldworker's familiarity with the particulars.

In the hands of most interpretive anthropologists, the insistence on the critical character of the details of cultural contexts for the understanding of any particular cultural phenomenon has carried an additional implication. Not only does the interpretation of specific cultural expressions require attention to their cultural settings, all cultural phenomena are fundamentally embedded in webs of significance so extensively and profoundly intertwined that analytical treatment can neither suitably extract these phenomena from their contexts nor formulate convincing generalizations about them in isolation. The upshot of all of this, which we have dubbed "hermeneutic exclusivism," is that the central prominence accorded contexts and their details has thoroughly discouraged theorizing about what seem to be widespread cross-cultural forms (such as religion). The webs of meaning in which we find ourselves suspended are, in fact, webs in which we find ourselves so *bound* as to preclude the possibility of explaining human behavior by means of general principles.

In the past fifteen years or so, versions of hermeneutic exclusivism have emerged that are even less friendly to explanatory theorizing. Since, on the hermeneutic view the study of culture is fundamentally interpretive, in recent years cultural anthropology has increasingly taken its inspiration from interpretive studies, instead of the sciences. Thus, postmodernism, reflexive anthropology, cultural constructivism and the like are less reactions *to* than apotheoses *of* the hermeneutic turn in anthropology. They permit what earlier hermeneutic exclusivists only dreamt that they could be.[3] On these models of inquiry, all cultural forms are, finally, texts—embodying forms of discourse— in need of interpretation. But interpretation itself is a never-ending process. "The constructivist view that culture is emergent, always alive and in process is widely accepted today ... what all proponents have in common is the view that the meaning of the text is not inherent in the text but emerges from how people read or experience the text" (Bruner 1994: 407). Crucially, those readings and experiences depend pivotally on the creativity, the resources, and, most important, the circumstances of the reader.

The valuable contributions of anthropologists of this stripe have been, first, to trace how various cultural forms render some readers and *their* experiences invisible (let alone more pernicious denials of their humanity) and, second, to highlight the resulting impoverishment of cultural inquiries. Where they have gone wrong, though, like their more conventionally hermeneutic predecessors, is in thinking that the creation and explication of increasingly wondrous webs of meaning exhausts cultural inquiry. We have argued elsewhere that this is only half of the story (see Lawson and McCauley 1990, 1995, and the section "The Hams in Anthropology" below). The resulting neglect of and disinterest in formulating systematic, empirically culpable theories on the part of postmodern cultural anthropology has created a vacuum that biological reductionists, such as sociobiologists, have been only too glad to occupy in the name of science.

It is exactly because they have failed to contest the notion that anthropologists own the concept 'culture' that scholars of religion have, for far too long, felt shy around their anthropological colleagues. By conceding 'culture' to the anthropologists, they have placed themselves either in the subservient position of passive recipients of anthropological reports or in the unenviable position of trying to match the anthropologists at their own game—by learning languages, performing fieldwork, and studying cultures' histories.[4] In light of the considerations we have raised in the previous paragraphs, matching anthropologists includes skillfully interpreting cultures at least and probably demonstrating ample sensitivity as well both to the ability of cultural forms to oppress—frequently in ways that are nearly invisible to most observers—and to the creative dimensions of individual experience in cultural transactions. However valuable these endeavors are, when pursuing them involves—as it so often does in their postmodern incarnations—eschewing overt attention to theories about cultural systems such as religion, they trap scholars of religion into conceding (1) that they cannot fruitfully study religious materials at any high level of abstraction either from their cultural settings, or from the wielding of power, or from the intimacy of personal experience and (2) that, therefore, religion is not subject to any penetrating cross-cultural analysis. These concessions undercut the long tradition of studying religion comparatively. In effect, then, exclusively pursuing interpretive endeavors in the study of religion plays right into the anthropologists' hand. It dooms scholars of religion to the status of anthropologists' half-prepared, junior colleagues (though such confusions about the character of the study of religion is nothing new—see Lawson and McCauley 1993).

Against such claims for the ownership of 'culture,' we hold that *on its own* cultural study *of this deeply interpretive sort* (whether by anthropologists or their imitators) hasn't enough theoretical capital to keep either the payments or the property up. Since it is too late to return 'culture' to the state of nature, we advise, at least, placing it in the public domain. We aim to contest the notion that anthropology either owns 'culture' or is capable of its purchase solely with coin of the interpretive realm.

In a recent article (Lawson and McCauley 1993), we criticized both religious studies and anthropology for assuming that concentrating on hermeneutics would insure both their methodological soundness and moral correctness. We argued that *cognitive* approaches to the study of religion are far more likely to achieve these goals. We also chastised scholars of religion for their confusions about the status of their own enterprise and argued that an exclusively humanistic program of religious studies relying only on interpretive techniques will render some religious phenomena virtually invisible. An exclusively hermeneutic approach is blind to certain religious phenomena that resist the hermeneuticists' textual metaphor. In actual practice accounts of religion as "textual" are finally distorting. (Ironically, the philosophical hermeneutics of Heidegger, Ricoeur, Gadamer, and others from which these analyses, at least in part, take their inspiration emphasize some of the forms and features of human praxis to which the interpretive analyses of anthropologists and scholars of comparative religion remain, all too often, inattentive.)

By contrast, in this paper we aim to reassure scholars of religion that they can escape these traps. Specifically, we hold (1) that scholars' cross-cultural insights about religion need not be suspect methodologically and (2) that religious systems can be studied comparatively. The crucial point, though, is that *these outcomes* require relaxing hermeneutic inclinations to subordinate, let alone eliminate, explanatory theorizing.

In the second section, we consider some implications for cultural anthropology of the current obsession with interpretive approaches to its materials. The anthropological search for meanings feeds on new information about ethnographic details and cultural settings. In such an atmosphere, fieldwork becomes an end in itself. *Being there* has become virtually sufficient for professional credentials. This professional focus places a premium on cultural diversity. Documenting the details of a culture that is largely like some other offers little interest. New, surprising, unexpected details are the fruit from which juicy new meanings are most easily squeezed.

But taste is a different matter. Too often interpretive anthropology neglects the theorizing necessary to distinguish the sweet fruits from the bitter. Theories of culture and culture's systems are pivotal for discriminating among the details, that is, for deciding which details *matter*. The most important role of fieldwork is to develop anthropological imagination and judgment— not merely to formulate new theories but to formulate *improved* theories. An anthropology that subordinates the formulation and evaluation of explanatory theories to the quest for ever-deeper meaning inevitably impoverishes itself.

The third section focuses on further implications of the hermeneutic approach to culture study. The most general implication reveals an important and suggestive asymmetry between the story *this version* of anthropology tells about itself and the stories the other social sciences tell about themselves. If the position of interpretive anthropologists' is right, at least when pushed to its logical extreme, then it looks as if the other social sciences (economics, political science, linguistics, etc.) have got things mostly wrong. The disproportionate emphasis on meanings and their critical dependence on cultural context renders the cross-cultural study of various cultural forms problematic.

We, then, briefly list in the last section some alternative approaches to 'culture.' There is, perhaps, no more telling evidence against claims about the ownership of culture than the fact that other disciplines have means for investigating the human world that seem to have clear implications about what is cultural. There are more ways to gain insight about culture than interminably cataloguing the details of one place after another.

The hams in anthropology

In his paper "The Stakes in Anthropology" Ernest Gellner (1988) suggests that American anthropology especially has become addicted to the search for meanings in cultural materials. Gellner echoes Dan Sperber's (1975) declarations that supplying interpretations of symbols' meanings compounds rather than solves the anthropologist's problems about symbolism. Meaning, in short, is the *problem*, not the solution. Gellner, however, recommends against the outright prohibition of further hermeneutical pursuits, since interpretive methods, when used with moderation, play a legitimate role in anthropological inquiry. Instead, Gellner proposes establishing Hermeneutics Anonymous—an organization devoted to encouraging sobriety in all matters meaningful. This would thwart the excesses of hermeneutic exclusivism.

All hermeneuticists see themselves as inhabiting a world of "texts," in which they propose minimally, to subordinate explanations to interpretations. Perhaps not all hermeneuticists have kidded themselves into believing that everything is a text, but they have unwittingly set the stage for such extravagant postmodernist claims (McCauley n.d.). Like Gellner, we suspect that such extravagance may undermine the very possibility of rational inquiry. At the very least, we think that hermeneuticists and postmodernists, by subordinating explanation to interpretation, overlook the productive interaction of interpretive and explanatory endeavors. We hold that the success of one *necessarily* depends upon the success of the other and, therefore, that subordinating explanation, let alone rejecting it the way hermeneutic exclusivists do, amounts to a fundamental misunderstanding of the generation of knowledge (Lawson and McCauley 1990: Chapter 1). We do *not* claim that searching for theoretical explanations of cultural phenomena that appeal to systematically related principles of general form is either the only or the premier ideal of inquiry in this domain, but we do hold that it should be subordinated to no other.

A scientific study of culture includes the search for its pervasive features, that is, so-called cultural universals, but, in fact, a cultural form or system need not be universal to be interesting theoretically. Within an evolutionary perspective on culture, cultural forms need not be universally distributed throughout the relevant population (any more than some biological trait needs to be universally distributed throughout a species). All cultures need not have capitalist economies for capitalist economies to be proper objects for theoretical inquiry and for economies generally to be sociocultural systems capable of isolation for analytical and explanatory purposes. Typically, "universals" simply refers to widespread cultural forms and systems, and on an evolutionary account that is all it need refer to.

From the standpoint of an evolutionary framework "[i]t is precisely the point of an explanatory theory to reduce diversity and to show in what manner it results from the encounter between general mechanisms, on the one hand, and many diverse circumstances on the other" (Boyer 1994: 7). The critical achievement is to specify the underlying mechanisms capable of generating the diversity of existing forms in interaction with assorted environments. In the biological case, the central mechanisms concern the replication and mutation of the genes—as this is shaped in the process of natural selection. In the cultural case we suspect that many, maybe most, of the pivotal mechanisms are psychological.

As in all science, such hypotheses direct empirical investigations into increasingly rarefied territories where they unearth anomalies that not only will not go away, but that constitute straightforward counter-instances to cherished hypotheses and assumptions. One of the reasons that fieldwork is so central to the training and credentialing of anthropologists is that fieldwork is what turns such anomalies up.

Fieldwork is difficult and demanding. Anthropologists often spend years in settings that are inhospitable and sometimes downright dangerous. They must not only avoid offending their hosts, they must develop sufficient rapport with them to obtain esoteric information about their culture. While coping with the unusual, they must also closely observe. Then, ideally at least, they must write about these often intimate experiences as if they are detached, "objective" observers (Geertz 1988: 10).

The presumption is that deep cross-cultural *understanding* depends upon *immersion* in some foreign setting. Cultural anthropologists earn their credentials by showing that after considerable work and effort they can render the exotic understandable. From learning a completely unfamiliar language to eating slugs and bugs, the difficulties of fieldwork exact a considerable toll. In light of that toll it should surprise no one that such immersion in an unfamiliar culture has become a necessary condition for professional authority in cultural anthropology.

What might come as a surprise, though, is that fieldwork has virtually also become a *sufficient* condition for professional authority. Attending closely to detail, admittedly integral to fieldwork, has developed a life of its own. To a considerable extent, the means have swallowed the end, the process has replaced the product. The hallmark of talks by young anthropologists anxious to demonstrate their competence is a slide show with a running commentary about invariably *small* details in the pictures that need not end up having any connections whatsoever. Reports of ethnographic details on the basis of firsthand experience have not only become a central foundation of professional authority, they have also become the necessary accoutrement to *any* discussion of cultural matters—whether or not those details are at all relevant to the cultural system in question. Traditional anthropology offers ample precedent. For example, what precisely *is* the point of Evans-Pritchard's picture of "youth and boy" (plate vii in *Nuer Religion*)? (See Geertz 1988.)

Interpretive anthropology has reduced the study of *culture* (by studying cultures) into the study of *cultures simpliciter*. An imbalance favoring interpretation over explanation has in the practice of the hermeneutic exclusivists evolved into an imbalance favoring ethnographic reporting over theorizing. Increasingly, cultural anthropology, even versions with overtly scientific aspirations, has tended to sacrifice the formulation of general theoretical proposals to the celebration of the details, the exaltation of the idiographic, and the veneration of the context. This encourages high-spirited symbolic anthropology, flush with resources for divining ever deeper layers of meaning in cultural materials.

One desideratum for distinguishing top-notch work from the also-ran is whether or not the details turn out to be surprising. If details are good, exotic details are better. They only seal the anthropologist's reputation as a skilled interpreter of culture. Like a good travel guide, the anthropologist renders the apparently baroque and bizarre understandable.

Ever since the discovery that some cultures do not possess the Western notion of modesty, the shock value associated with documenting cultural diversity has hardly diminished. Most anthropologists, though, are not so benighted by postmodernist excess as to have lost *all* sight of scientific possibilities. Fortunately, their interest in the unusual does not merely reflect a penchant for showmanship but their persisting but, all too often, suppressed concern with science as well. Exotic details are exotic because they challenge explicitly formulated hypotheses about general features of culture or, perhaps even more significantly, because they defy tacit presumptions we all bring to our reflections on alien cultures. But exotic details are even more interesting when they prove just as susceptible to some theory's analysis as do far more familiar cultural phenomena. These days, though, professional fame does not ordinarily accrue to the researcher who suggests that the apparently fantastic is actually commonplace—that it is nothing but a further manifestation of cultural dynamics some theory has rendered familiar in contexts closer to home. Emerging from the bush only to report that some little known group is a lot more like us than meets the eye is not fashionable.

Roger Keesing offered grounds for hesitation about becoming entranced with bizarre details, noting that "[a]nthropologists, with their predilections for the exotic and their predispositions toward, even vested interests in, depicting cultures as radically different from ours and from one another, are prone to choose readings that fit these expectations and interests" (1987: 162). Keesing cautioned against reading too much into other peoples' conventions for talking about their experiences and mental lives. He argued that the more theoretically significant discovery would be to learn that broad cultural diversity rests on fairly mundane processes. Keesing cited, for example, Lakoff and Johnson (1980) who account for pervasive structuring of experience in terms of relatively simple metaphoric comparisons, many of which arise from basic bodily experiences that all human beings share (e.g., construing anger in terms of contained heat—typically, the heat of a *fluid* in a container).

The cognitive approach to religious materials that we have pursued employs the same sort of abstemiousness concerning symbols and their interpretations. Not only do such cognitive analyses explain some aspects of cultural diversity and creativity in terms of the perfectly ordinary, but they also delineate features of the underlying cognitive mechanisms responsible for the phenomena in question. In *Rethinking Religion*, for example, we have shown how participants' representations of religious rituals piggyback on quite common cognitive means for the representation of actions generally. We also specify a relatively small collection of principles that capture the representational capacities employed (1990: Chapter 5). Pascal Boyer's *The Naturalness of Religious Ideas* (1994) provides further (and numerous) arguments and illustrations of how thoroughly normal patterns of cognitive development can bear most of the explanatory responsibility for the retention, recurrence, and perpetuation of the various unusual, "counter-intuitive" commitments characteristic of religious systems.

Scientific progress always involves an ongoing interaction between theorizing and attending to observational detail. *The trick is in knowing what details count.* When identifying the most prominent achievements in the history of science, the focus reliably falls on the development of particular theories and the startling observational findings and experimental results they provoked. We know that neither the ages nor the colors nor the atmospheric contents nor the thermal properties of the planets have anything to do with either the explanation or prediction of their relative motions, because of the success of the theory Isaac Newton formulated that identifies the important variables.

Excessive interest in detail for its own sake has caused anthropology to lose its moorings, because it has led it to neglect theorizing. Neglecting theory is deadly from a scientific standpoint, because *it is precisely the confrontation of competing theories that determines which details matter.* Consequently, the theories with which scientists operate, whether consciously or not, determine which details will receive attention.

Sir Arthur Eddington undertook his famous expedition at considerable expense far from the shores of Great Britain, because the concern to rationally adjudicate the conflict between two of the most important physical theories in human history, namely classical mechanics and special relativity, required the observation of a very specific celestial event which was only possible at very specific points on the globe at very specific times. The *conflict between these two theories* made the apparent positions of stars in the sky close to the sun during its eclipse *important details* for deciding which of the two better organized a vast array of physical phenomena that extend *far beyond the specific events observed* by Eddington. It is not as if in the first decades of this century scientists did not already know a great deal about the sun and its eclipses, about light and its propagation, and about stars, gravitation and a host of other related celestial and physical phenomena! All of that knowledge, though, did not include *the details that were critical for advancing knowledge at this juncture.*

Second generation fieldworkers would not have much to do, if the first generation had all the right theories and, therefore, had focused on all of the right details. Not coincidentally, the hallmark of second generation fieldwork is revisionism. Revisionists approach the previously studied culture with alternative hypotheses in virtue of which they ascertain that their predecessors either organized the details incorrectly, focused on the wrong details, missed critical details (that the new hypotheses authenticate), or some combination of these three.

A further problem with the veneration of context and the resulting neglect of explicit theory is that the theoretical perspectives informing these revisionists' judgments are not usually the objects of direct reflection and, thus, are often not even consciously entertained. Without open recognition of the underlying theoretical competition at stake, these disagreements look like unmotivated or (worse) ideologically motivated squabbles about the facts. Absent the self-conscious comparison of theories, second generation fieldworkers are simply vying for the professional limelight. The stakes in anthropology are too rare to settle for mere hams.

If fieldwork and the knowledge of cultural details it fosters become the ends of anthropological research, then it will be the end of anthropological research.

From the standpoint of a social *science*, celebrating contextual details is just not enough. Such details may provide the means for assessing existing theories; however, their nearly uninhibited celebration has eclipsed two fundamental tasks critical to advancing the understanding of culture.

We have already touched upon the first. As a result of this overwhelming focus on the idiographic, anthropologists too often hold their theoretical presumptions unreflectively, which is to say, although they bring biases to their fieldwork experience, they have little understanding of their genesis, rationale, or organization (if any exists). Theories organize inquiry; explicit theories organize inquiry explicitly. The problem is that, all things being equal, it is better to hold positions reflectively rather than unreflectively in order both to decrease the sort of squabbling described above and to increase the efficiency, the productivity, and the civility of anthropological discussion.

Second, and perhaps even more important, this proclivity of anthropology has also obscured the obligation of scientists to speculate, that is, to formulate *new* theories. Scientists do not study the details of the world merely to assess existing claims about it. If that were the only point, such study would have ceased long ago. For as Kuhn (1970), Feyerabend (1975), and other philosophers of science have noted, every theory, from its inception, faces counter-instances. Science does not progress in any simple-minded way. Theories are more resilient than metal ducks in a shooting gallery. They do not flop over from the glancing hits of occasional counter-instances. Social science, in particular, requires the informed judgments of experienced inquirers—looking behind the appearances, sifting through the facts, marshalling their practical knowledge, considering and ranking alternatives by both judging and weighing divergent evidence, explanatory power, relative scope, suggestiveness, simplicity, and more (Thagard 1992). This is why fieldwork experience is so often helpful.

We have nothing against gathering information from the field, and we fully recognize that theoretical proposals about cultural systems must answer to the ethnographic facts. But we also subscribe to the well-worn hermeneutical insight that experience and conceptual schemes (and observation and theories) are interdependent. The point, in short, is that what facts matter and where researchers look for them is a function of an ongoing negotiation between the theoretician and the ethnographer operating as *equal* partners.

Finally, the most important motive for fieldwork is neither its ability to arm the ethnographer with counter-instances with which to club prominent theories nor even its ability to corroborate preferred theories but rather its role in educating the anthropological imagination. The progress of science turns not on the proliferation of *mere* speculation but on the proliferation of *informed* speculation. Researchers' familiarity with the facts and their considered judgment are what inform speculations. Those speculations typically take the form of inferences to the best explanation (Peirce's "abductive inference"). From these origins, more sophisticated theories take shape. The continuing goal is not only to formulate new theories but to formulate *better* theories on the basis of the comparative insights that fieldwork provokes.

Fieldworkers provide thick and intricate descriptions firmly rooted in firsthand knowledge of the details of different ways of life. The hope is that these analyses will divulge patterns of sufficiently general significance to aid understanding in other cultural settings. The danger of analyses so firmly rooted in particular circumstances is precisely that they resist generalization. Hence, as Geertz (1988) has noted, anthropologists face a rhetorical dilemma, if not a logical one. They must display their intimate knowledge of the ethnographic details while demonstrating that the analyses that emerge from that intimate knowledge do not hang on it essentially.

Another limitation of this approach is that *the details go on forever*. Most limitations on and uniformity in the details of ethnographic reports are overwhelmingly a function of common general assumptions that virtually all anthropologists operate with (largely unconsciously) about what matters in a culture (kinship, social roles, rituals, myths, legitimacy, traditions, and more). We should emphasize straightaway that *we do not begrudge them these assumptions*! On the contrary, they are the ultimate sources of most telling ethnographic comparisons. The problem is that fieldworkers who are not explicitly aware of these theoretical assumptions and their implications have no clear guidelines for determining which details count and when they can stop collecting them. The satisfactoriness of a description is always judged relative to a theory. Thus, for example, because we have proposed a theory of religious ritual (Lawson and McCauley 1990) that employs some assumptions at odds with those many cultural anthropologists prefer, we have found that, despite the myriad details of their ethnographic reports, they frequently do not contain much critical information that is relevant to the questions we are asking.

Although anthropology holds novices' feet to the fieldwork fires, the discipline seems considerably less vigilant about practitioners' subsequent works once they have been initiated. Comparative ethnographic studies have been known to report on groups with which the authors have had no direct encounters. Geertz, for example, notes that Ruth Benedict had no firsthand experience with two of the three groups she discussed in *Patterns of Culture* (Geertz 1988: 112). Her reputation secured, Benedict was professionally free to pursue *comparative* ethnography.

The crucial point is that we have just been sketching a case for why this is *perfectly acceptable*—if the inquiry is overtly theoretical (as opposed to intimately ethnographic only). Once you know what a science of culture should do, you don't have to visit every place under the sun. Armed with a theory about patterns of culture or about the dynamics of some specific cultural system, the investigator has a clear view of the facts that matter. Objections to such projects that argue that their discussions of specific cases fail to meet the standards for description touted in ethnographic circles obsessed with context and preoccupied with details are not compelling. Where a theory has a grip, the details that matter are those that contribute to the elaboration and evaluation of it and its competitors.

By now, we assume it is clear that we are criticizing *a specific vision* of cultural anthropology that we regard as impoverished. In effect, we are suggesting that even the projects of scientifically minded cultural anthropologists have largely been co-opted by the agendas of postmodernists and thick describers. This dominant vision of cultural anthropology neglects the formulation and improvement of theory in favor of preoccupations with the collection of ethnographic detail and the specification of cultural settings. Entranced by the never-ending search for deeper and deeper meanings, interpretive anthropology has largely devolved into a cultural freak show. Its emphasis on documenting *apparent* cultural diversity (how can we know it is *genuine* diversity without the guidance of a successful theory that provides criteria for distinguishing cultural types?) has been so single-minded that interpretive anthropology and its postmodern descendants have largely abandoned their epistemic obligations to formulate better theories.

The prima donna of the social sciences

We suggested in the previous section that no one owns the concept of 'culture' and that the most progressive explanatory theories of cultural phenomena available should determine that concept's fate. Just like the concept of 'heredity' in biology, accounts of contributing mechanisms and systems will constrain the fate of the concept 'culture.' That anthropology has tried to reserve 'culture' for itself is troubling enough. That interpretive visionaries have picked up on this claim is even more bothersome. In this section, we shall further explore the consequences of those visionaries' views.

Insisting that cultural phenomena can only be understood as embedded in webs of meanings carries an interesting implication for the place of anthropology among the social sciences. Pushed to its extreme—which is exactly where some of these visionaries (especially some of the cultural constructivists) have pushed it[5]—this insistence on the preeminence of the idiographic sets anthropology apart from and ahead of the other social sciences. Plowing through its part, anthropology of this sort hopes to hog the social scientific stage, not merely oblivious to the other members of the company but actively trying to shove them into the wings.

The central argument runs as follows. *The* key to understanding any cultural phenomenon is to ascertain its meaning(s). The particulars of their contexts determine the meanings of cultural items. Hence, every cultural matter is *inextricably* tied to the particulars of its context. Therefore, regarding particular cultural phenomena merely as tokens of cultural types is importantly misleading and abstracting general cultural forms for the purposes of cross-cultural theorizing is intrinsically wrong-headed.

We have argued at length both in the previous section and elsewhere (Lawson and McCauley 1990: Chapter 1) against this argument's first premise. Our current goal is not to repeat or develop those arguments, but rather to provide an additional argument by highlighting what is a not-too-often-recognized and a not-too-palatable (let alone popular) consequence of this view. The view of research on sociocultural phenomena embodied in the argument's conclusions condemns precisely what all of the other social sciences aim to do. In short, if these anthropologists are right, then virtually all the other social sciences are wrong.

Economics, political science, linguistics, and sociology (more generally) all suppose (1) that some social and cultural systems (economies, political systems, languages, etc.) are isolable as theoretical objects *independently* of contextual variability, (2) that the assorted examples of such systems across a wide expanse of cultural settings share various features that are pivotal to their explanation, and (3) that this fact alone is sufficient to justify their analytical abstraction from their specific cultural contexts. Psychology makes the same presumptions about human psyches. Each of these inquiries is committed to the view that the forces operating within these systems are sufficiently robust across cultures (or across individuals in the case of psychology) that many features of these systems can be described and explained in relative isolation.

Presumably, it is clear by now that *here* we side unequivocally with these other social sciences. Pushed to its logical extreme, the interpretivists' position implies that the other social sciences are wrong-headed, if not impossible (McCauley n.d.). It would prohibit all general proposals about the dynamics of markets, the distribution of power, and the formal features of languages (let alone the structures of religious systems—which interest us). If the distinctiveness of everything cultural turns on webs of culturally specific meaning[6] in which those things figure, then attempts to isolate and generalize about such systems must prove fundamentally mistaken.

As we have just hinted, this position has direct implications for the study of religion and explains why contemporary anthropologists are often skeptical about the possibility of developing theories about *specifically religious phenomena* (Boyer 1994: 37). Ironically, prior to hermeneutics' heyday, anthropologists—as the overseers of 'culture'—had quite different motives for resisting theories of specific cultural systems such as religion. Instead of rejecting such theorizing outright, they feared that the success of such theories would shut down their show. Their worry was that the triumph of such explanatory theories—about religious ritual, for example, in isolation from larger concerns about other ritualized cultural forms—would render their peculiarly *cultural* analyses superfluous.[7] (We hold that this worry was and is ungrounded. It underestimates the value of *any* even moderately successful proposal that gains some explanatory purchase. The ignorance about sociocultural matters is considerable enough to tolerate multiple theoretical approaches at many different levels of specificity.)

A further motive, with which we are *sympathetic,* was some anthropologists' concern to demonstrate that there was nothing unique about either religious systems or religious experience (as manifestations of a cultural form, in particular). We have nothing against such deflationary approaches—so long as they provide their own explanations of the phenomena in question *and* provide explanations of why the religious *appears* to be so different from other cultural forms on some fronts. We conceive of our own position as one that offers a (comparatively) deflationary account of religious ritual, but one that aspires to *explain* the appearances rather than deny them.

So, whether on traditional grounds of the primacy of *cultural* analysis and deflationary views of religious phenomena or on more recent grounds concerning entangled webs of meaning, anthropologists have remained antagonistic to the theoretical isolation of specific cultural forms for the purposes of cross-cultural explanation. The current version of the argument jeopardizes the possibility of theorizing about religion in the same way that it threatens the projects of the other social sciences. If all religious materials are only properly understood in all of their cultural connectedness, then religion stands little chance of independent theoretical analysis as a recognizable cultural form.

In *Rethinking Religion* we unwaveringly insisted that religious systems and religious ritual systems, in particular, enjoy sufficient distinctiveness and robustness across a variety of cultural settings to serve as the objects of independent theoretical analyses. We have contended that such analyses of religious systems will involve explanations carried out in the same sort of *relative* isolation from the variable details of context that pertains in any other science.

Not surprisingly, most anthropologists seem to think that no compelling reasons exist for distinguishing religious ritual from rituals of other types. By contrast, we maintain that religious ritual systems can be usefully isolated *across* cultures for the purposes of explanatory theorizing and prediction. Note, our view does not preclude the possibility that religious rituals are largely continuous with other sorts of ritualized behaviors.[8] Indeed, we argue that on some theoretically important fronts religious rituals are continuous with *all* forms of action (Lawson and McCauley 1990: Chapter 5). The important point, though, is that without a theory of ritual-in-general that matches our theory's precision, systematicity, generality, and empirical tractability, we see no reason to defer to anthropologists' unsystematic intuitions here.

Such issues are not decided *a priori*. Finally, whether theories of religious systems (and theories of any sort) deserve social scientists' respect turns on those theories' relative productivity and empirical success. In scientific contexts, explanatory and predictive successes are the final measures of all things. Why should anthropology not embrace a theory that brings *some* cross cultural order to at least one recognizable subset of ritual materials? Reluctance on this front is a function of that same exaggerated reverence for detail that we have been challenging throughout this paper.

Our suggestion, then, is that the study of religion will prove most appropriately and most productively situated among the social sciences (understood broadly to include the psychological and cognitive sciences). The specific theoretical strategies we are exploring take their cues from work in the cognitive sciences. Although this is a pioneering research concerning religious ritual systems, analyses of other cultural systems along cognitive lines have arisen in both linguistics (Lakoff 1987; Langacker 1987) and anthropology (Sperber 1975; Boyer 1993, 1994). The study of religion, like the studies of language, economy, and power can stand as an identifiable subdiscipline within the overall social scientific enterprise. Successful theorizing in each of these subdisciplines contributes to our knowledge of culture.

The concept of 'culture' is as notoriously vague as cultures themselves are notoriously difficult to study. Such problems are not news in science. 'culture' is no worse off than the concepts 'mind' or 'species' or 'chemical bond.' The way scientists *always* proceed with such problems is to study their empirically tractable features and subsystems. Not only does anthropology not own the concept of culture, the lesson of the physical, biological, and psychological sciences suggests that its development will likely depend upon progress in those social sciences concerned with culture's "constituents," that is, the various theoretically isolable systems that make up culture.

Coda

Probably no consideration more clearly reveals the emptiness of cultural anthropology's proprietary claims than the fact that other disciplines have developed means for investigating the world that bear directly on how we conceive of culture. Neither anthropological suppositions nor anthropological methods are *necessary* for either collecting empirical evidence or drawing conclusions about the character of culture. These other types of biological, psychological, social, and cultural inquiry have revealed new ways to approach the topics of culture and cultural forms from angles unlike those typically employed in cultural anthropology (see, for example, Lumsden and Wilson 1981 or Tooby and Cosmides 1989). Specifically, they include drawing some empirically informed conclusions about cultural matters without documenting every little detail about each and every spot on God's green earth.

Three areas of research come immediately to mind—concerning nonhuman primates, early childhood development, and various sorts of social and cognitive impairments. The first two involve phenomena that enjoy some continuity with the behavior of enculturated, adult *Homo sapiens*—the first, evolutionary and the second, developmental. They provide perspective on both organisms' intrinsic capacities that require little (if any) cultural input and possible biological origins of cultural forms. The third area of research exploits a well-worn strategy in the biological sciences, viz., to gain understanding about normal functioning by studying pathologies. Injuries and breakdowns offer both impetus to study and useful information about a mechanism's routine functioning. These three areas of research not only arise from sciences we have touted elsewhere, but the sorts of evidence involved spring from studies that are far more precise and controlled than most of the data available by means of conventional research in cultural anthropology.

Space limitations require that we but briefly list an example of each. When Sue Savage-Rumbaugh and her collaborators (1986) found that the pygmy chimpanzee, Kanzi, both comprehended a fair amount of spoken English and appropriately responded on the basis of mere exposure to other animals' training sessions, we learned that the spontaneous acquisition of symbols, let alone their use, was not confined to human beings.

Frank Keil's research (1979, 1989) on young children's appreciation of basic ontological distinctions strongly suggests that their representation of many concepts is subject to little, if any, cultural variability. Presumably, mastery of these distinctions is so pivotal to getting on in the world that their acquisition is either rooted in our biology or *necessitated* by circumstance.

In the course of developing an account of the unique features of what they contend is "cultural learning," Tomasello et al. (1993) examine evidence concerning autism. They predict that because most autistic persons do not conceive of others as what they call "reflective agents," they will often be incapable of acquiring various sorts of cultural knowledge. Although the criteria for diagnosing autism are by no means uncontroversial, Tomasello and his colleagues note that approximately half of the persons so diagnosed prove incapable of acquiring language.

It is, in addition to developmental psychology, various subdisciplines of the cognitive sciences that we (and Boyer) have mined for the study of religious systems, including theoretical and cognitive linguistics and social and cognitive psychology (see too Baranowski 1994). The mutual penetration of mind and culture encourages disciplinary cross-talk. Some cultural anthropologists have begun to consult the cognitive sciences as a means of exploring the influences of culture on mind. Shore (1995), for example, considers culturally specific schemas that organize multiple areas of participants' experience. By contrast our major interest has been in the influence of mind on culture. We have focused on what the cognitive sciences reveal both about the study of the mind generally and about the constraints the particularly human version of mentality exerts on cultural forms.

Thus, the cognitive sciences provide both methodological and substantive inspiration. For example, on the methodological front, we enlisted a host of strategic resources theoretical linguistics employs for theorizing about cultural competencies—exploiting an analogy between the competencies of native speakers with their natural languages and of ritual participants with their religious ritual systems (see McCauley and Lawson 1993).

Substantively, research in the relevant fields suggests cognitive constraints on and contributions to those cultural competencies. Findings in the cognitive sciences concerning concept representation, memory dynamics, social attribution, and conceptions of agency—to name only some of the most prominent considerations—offer valuable hints about *why* cultural forms such as religious beliefs and religious rituals take the shapes that they do and about *how* they operate and persist as cultural systems.

Moreover, these cognitive considerations typically apply *regardless of the meanings attributed to these cultural forms*. While acknowledging the role of interpretation in advancing our knowledge of culture, such theoretical approaches as we are recommending generate systematic insights about cultural forms without preoccupation with their meanings. The point is not to silence the interpretivists but to reclaim a role for scientific theorizing in the study of culture—releasing it from *any* proprietary claims and leaving it in the hands of the most productive and penetrating explanatory schemes available. Finally, no one owns 'culture,' because in science our best explanatory schemes face relentless pressure to improve.

Overcoming Barriers to a Cognitive Psychology of Religion

Introduction

The aims of this paper are to identify three barriers to the development of cognitive approaches to the study of religion and to suggest how each might be circumvented. The first of these barriers is methodological and lurks amid two issues that, historically, have dominated anthropologists' reflections on the relationship of their discipline to psychology. The older of the two can be characterized as the "psychic unity" controversy (see Shore 1995). The second issue is the controversy over the "autonomy of culture." Advocates of the latter thesis are usually unsympathetic to psychological explanations of religious phenomena. In the section "Cognitive Unity or Cultural Autonomy?," I shall begin by briefly examining each of those issues and then exploring the connections between the two as well as interesting logical tensions that arise in the face of popular responses to each. In the section "The Commonplace and the Cognitive," I shall consider a pair of barriers to a cognitive psychology of religion rooted in two strategies that have dominated many psychologists' approaches to the study of religion. I will argue that for some purposes, at least, both strategies should be relaxed. Finally, in the section "Advantages of a Competence Approach to Religious Materials," I shall briefly sketch one sort of cognitive approach to religious phenomena, suggesting how it handles the two strategic barriers in particular.

Cognitive unity or cultural autonomy?

The psychic unity controversy revolves around the question of whether all members of our species have roughly the same psychological make-up (and cognitive equipment) or not. From its inception, anthropology has faced the problem of explaining the substantial divergences of cultures with respect to their scientific, technological, and institutional achievements. No doubt, differences in natural environments play some role. Still, accounting for such disparities, at least in part, on the basis of different cognitive profiles has always been a standard explanatory strategy.

Not unlike missionaries' periodic visits to their home churches, much of anthropology's charm has turned on providing academic colleagues with reports about the odd ways other folks seem to think. The *huge* number of such reports provides an evidential force that largely eliminates the suspicions that scattered anecdotes would engender. Moreover, on some relevant fronts, cross-cultural psychological experiments offer evidence supporting anthropologists' claims about the diversity of cognitive styles and strategies used in different cultures (Cole and Scribner 1974; Scribner and Cole 1981).

The critical question concerns the salient variable(s) responsible for these different patterns of thought. The controversy surrounding the apparent cognitive *dis*unity anthropologists have documented concerns just how deeply it goes. Are anthropologists reporting on the impact of cultural variation on cognitive style or on differences whose origins reside in the biology of different human groups? Do different peoples think differently because their varying cultures shape them so or because they differ biologically? Finally, are differences in cognitive strategies rooted in cultural or biological variation?

Each of the two principal responses has its drawbacks. The logic of biological explanations *seems* clear enough initially, though usually the intention is to explain putative differences in native cognitive *abilities* rather than cognitive *strategies*. The intellectual efforts devoted to establishing the cognitive superiority or inferiority of one racially or ethnically defined group or another has had a long and undistinguished history (Gould 1981). The point is not just a political one. The difficulties associated with clarifying the central concepts, employing and interpreting statistical measures properly, ascertaining the import of the myriad empirical findings the various parties to such discussions deem relevant, and fathoming the sheer complexity of the psychological and biological research should suffice both to belie the apparent simplicity of such biological explanations and to give partisans considerable pause about any of their conclusions (Neisser et al. 1996).

In the nineteenth century, most of the founders of anthropology subscribed to the biological unity of humankind, accounting for the differences between cultures in terms of cultural evolution. Basically, on this view Western cultures had reached more progressive stages in the process of cultural evolution than had those outside the West. Although significant biological differences might not be responsible for Western development, Western culture was presumed not only to be more developed but also to possess a superior arsenal of intellectual tools by virtue of which it was more developed.

For a host of reasons, not the least of which was an emerging appreciation in the course of fieldwork of the intellectual sophistication of non-Western peoples, anthropologists in this century have largely abandoned arguments for the psychic unity of humankind that rely on appeals to stages of cultural evolution to explain cognitive diversity. Nonetheless, most cultural anthropologists in this century have resisted biological accounts of cognitive variation. To do so is neither to affirm a contradiction nor to deny the cognitive diversity to which anthropologists have continued to give testimony but, rather, to adopt either or both of two positions.

Boas (1963) was an early advocate of the first; in fact, he endorsed both. Focusing on the configurations of material and historical arrangements unique to each culture, Boas and many cultural anthropologists since affirm some form of cultural relativism, holding that cultures are not more or less advanced; they are just different. The fitness of a culture is no more absolute than the fitness of an organism. Judgments about the adequacy of some cultural form are always relative to the context. Each culture is a product of the particular constellation of conditions and historical circumstances in which it has developed. The differences between cultures and their associated cognitive styles pose no threat to claims for an underlying psychic and cognitive unity, because the various patterns that arise are adaptations to specific natural and cultural environments.

The second position, of which even Levy-Bruhl qualifies as an advocate, affirms the reality of cognitive diversity, but insists that it is, indeed, overwhelmingly, if not exclusively, a product of culture. Different social and cultural circumstances produce different cognitive outcomes. Human groups of comparable sizes exhibit comparable biological variation. To avoid the appearance of begging the question in the face of the biological option, that is, the claim that the correct explanation of divergent cognitive styles across cultures is rooted in biological variation, advocates of this second position, presumably, must maintain that any biologically unimpaired human could acquire other cultures' patterns of thought given the right circumstances.

To some extent, anthropologists' very ability to report on other cultures' cognitive styles presumes precisely that. With all the appropriate *ceteris paribus* clauses in place, the claim is that any normal human being could have learned any culture's patterns of thought, if he or she had been suitably enculturated. Important evidence for the truth of this counter-factual is that many people *do* seem to learn other cultures' ways of thinking, even when all things are not equal (see, for example, Barth 1987: 75, 88).

In explaining cognitive diversity, the number of complications accompanying the biological option may only be exceeded by the number accompanying this cultural one. The central concepts are largely the same, and it is no easier to draw hard distinctions differentiating particular cultures within the morass of cultural variation than it is to draw them about races or ethnic groups amid the perplexities biological variation presents. Of course, issues concerning the application and interpretation of statistical measures and the range of empirical findings the various parties deem relevant also remain unchanged. So, if cultural accounts enjoy an advantage, it would, presumably, inhere in their theoretical underpinnings, their investigative methods, or their research designs. Unfortunately, these seem just the fronts where sociocultural investigations typically exhibit relatively less precision, penetration, and verisimilitude than the natural sciences. Nowhere in science is the gap greater between the problems that animate inquiries and the models and methods that address them than in the study of social and cultural systems.

That gap has only encouraged hermeneutically inclined anthropologists and their postmodern brethren (advocates of what I shall hereafter call "pan-hermeneutics"). Having foresworn anthropology's long-standing aspirations to scientific respectability in the study of culture, these anthropologists find *solace* in this gap. They eschew searches for explanatory mechanisms, championing, instead, the following two positions: (1) some variation on the old autonomy of culture thesis, that is, the claim that fundamentally cultural concepts ("power" is the current favorite) are necessary and sufficient for the analysis of cultural phenomena and (2) some version of cultural constructivism, that is, the claim that cultural forces construct not just *meanings* but *realities* out of the material and psychic substratum (see, for example, White 1992).

This newest line of defense for the autonomy of culture thesis diverges from its predecessors in that it buys the analytical authority of cultural concepts at the cost of surrendering cultural anthropology's explanatory pretensions. The uniqueness of each cultural setting makes the interpretation of the meanings and realities cultures create analysis enough. A few comments are in order.

First, I recognize that many postmodern cultural anthropologists may not grant (or even recognize) the coincidences of their positions with either the autonomy of culture movement or hermeneutic approaches. Nor are they likely to acknowledge the nearly direct descent of postmodernism from the latter. Second, this discussion of the autonomy of culture thesis does *not* concern loyalty to a particular school of thought (emanating largely from the University of Chicago a few decades back) but rather a *position* to which, I would maintain, both interpretive and postmodern cultural anthropologists are committed (whether they realize it or not) no less than that earlier group was.

Third, ironically, their roots in hermeneutic approaches notwithstanding, many contemporary postmodern anthropologists' preoccupations with power relations implicitly presuppose the possibility of *explaining* cultural phenomena. Usually, though, they seem neither to realize or acknowledge this implication nor particularly interested in either refining or testing the explanatory hypothesis they advance, viz., that all cultural arrangements, finally, can be explained exclusively in terms of the distribution and exercise of power (*culturally* conceived) (Nuckolls 1995). Without either the means for or the expectation of refining and testing such hypotheses, a discipline constantly risks devolving into ideology.

The spirit that informs the wielding of such blunt instruments for the analysis of sociocultural phenomena seems contrary both to the anti-reductionistic commitments of these postmodern cultural anthropologists and to the entire discipline's preoccupations with detail and cultural uniqueness. Sweeping theories of this sort often gain adherents, but rarely, if ever, undergo much amendment in the face of contrary evidence.

Still, the point of this discussion is not to challenge the prevailing ideology in cultural anthropology on every front, but rather to explore the logical tensions underlying simultaneous commitments (consciously recognized or not) to

(a) the possibility of systematically explaining sociocultural phenomena, (b) the autonomy of culture thesis, and (c) the psychic unity thesis. Interestingly, I think that most postmodern accounts of culture in terms of power relations are implicitly pledged to all three. (As I suggested above, they are not likely to confess to either thesis [a] or [b].) Even if I am wrong about that, though, my main objectives are to convince anthropologists and scholars of religion who *are* committed to all three (1) that recent psychological and cognitive science has produced methods and findings that will illuminate sociocultural phenomena and, thus, (2) that they should surrender thesis (b).

Virtually all of contemporary cultural anthropologists do, indeed, subscribe to the psychic unity thesis as well. Thus, they affirm the centrality of human beings' common biological readiness to acquire whatever culture they find themselves in (at least before achieving some critical developmental thresholds). They also reject proposals that promote biological bases of cognitive and cultural differences.

While generally supporting the values that inform these positions and happily acknowledging culture's role in shaping many meanings and realities, not only do I see no need to press any autonomy claims in behalf of either culture or cultural analyses, I regard them as counterproductive. However, it has not generally been the autonomy of culture thesis that has worried the scientifically oriented dissenters in recent anthropology. Over the decades, anthropologists have offered many arguments in its defense. The deeper and perfectly legitimate concern of anthropologists who still seek general explanations has been with the relativism so many of their colleagues enthusiastically embrace. The relativism that results from the overwhelming emphasis on the contextual and the idiographic and that characterizes the Boasian legacy, hermeneutics, and cultural constructivism in anthropology constitutes a substantial epistemic burden—a burden that anthropologists who retain serious comparative ambitions, let alone general explanatory ambitions, should find difficult to bear. Without at least some low-level theorizing systematically connecting some cultural features with one another, both comparative and explanatory projects risk being cast adrift in a sea of random details.

Still, anthropologists unwilling to swallow either extreme versions of cultural relativism or their epistemic consequences have not felt chary about the autonomy of culture thesis. Three considerations, discussed in order of *increasing* importance, should make us wary, though.

First, underlying the more recent pan-hermeneutic rendering of the cultural account of cognitive diversity is a strikingly traditional view about where most of the explanatory action resides—and, interestingly, it is *not* at the cultural level. The cultural autonomy thesis maintains the necessity and sufficiency of cultural phenomena to account for (other) cultural phenomena. Explanations of cognitive diversity should appeal to cultural forces and forms. So far, so good. But, interestingly, on the psychic unity thesis cognitive diversity becomes a comparatively superficial fact, at least from an *explanatory* standpoint. The underlying biological unity of the species and the capacities that biology endows do the primary explanatory work. Neonates are biologically prepared to acquire whatever culture they find themselves in. In its explanatory assumptions at least, the heart of the twentieth-century version of the psychic unity thesis has a surprisingly biological beat. Culture's effects, by comparison, are, apparently, little better than unsystematic.

Cultural constructivism does not circumvent this problem. That position simply advances an even stronger version of the cultural autonomy thesis. Cultural constructivism insists not only that analyses employing exclusively cultural terms can account for cultural phenomena but also that many phenomena that are typically discussed at lower levels of analysis (e.g., the emotions) are, in fact, the results of cultural forces. However, such accounts are utterly implausible precisely when explananda concern phenomena which cultural variables do not constrain. That, of course, is expressly the assumption about the psychic unity thesis.

Still, this first consideration has the feel of debates about half-full and half-empty glasses. The second concern is more serious. The comparative superficiality of the phenomena, ultimately, is not nearly as important as the comparative superficiality of proposed explanations for it. Behind these concerns is a basic question regarding the logic of a *cultural* explanation.

Recall that pursuing the cultural option with respect to cognitive profiles is to declare that the variation to be explained is cultural, not biological. The cultural autonomy thesis requires that explanations of this variation proceed on cultural terms. Absent detailed accounts of the cultural mechanisms involved, though, such explanations inevitably look extremely thin. Citing variations in specific cultures provides little explanatory grip on the divergence of their associated cognitive profiles, if those sundry profiles are *themselves* construed merely as further examples of *cultural variation*. More generally, the thickness of cultural descriptions is typically *inversely* proportional to that of cultural explanations. Such thoroughly cultural explanations are, all too often, insufficiently theoretical, that is, their central concepts do not diverge much from those employed in the descriptions of the explananda. It was just this dearth of detailed theoretical accounts of cultural *mechanisms* that "identify causal links, and not mere correlations or isomorphies" (Barth 1987: 55) as well as the gap between existing models and the phenomena they address that has so reassured the pan-hermeneuticists about their adoption of the autonomy of culture thesis and about their disinterest in the standing of their proposals as scientific explanations.

We have two objections born of this second consideration: (1) that proposed cultural explanations of irreducibly cultural phenomena that contain no theoretical proposals about the cultural mechanisms involved are *un*likely to achieve much explanatory leverage and (2) that the cultural autonomy thesis encourages discounting just those investigations (in psychology and biology) most likely to stimulate fruitful anthropological theorizing about such mechanisms. More generally, not only does the cultural autonomy thesis restrict the form of acceptable explanations of cultural phenomena, it also discourages scholars from looking in just those quarters perhaps most likely to suggest useful explanatory theories. In short, the thesis imposes constraints on acceptable cultural explanations that greatly increase the probability that the proposals it permits will prove comparatively shallow.

This leads directly to the third consideration. One common strategy in science for explaining correlations discovered at one level of analysis, especially when no theoretically suggestive models have arisen at that level, is to inquire about the explanatory resources available at lower levels of analysis. This amounts to searching for an underlying mechanism producing the observed patterns (see Lawson and McCauley 1990: 177–180; Bechtel and Richardson 1993). The problem for so many cultural anthropologists here, though, is that this would seem to be tantamount to abandoning the commitment to cultural analysis in favor of either psychology or biology. Such "reductionistic" options are nonstarters for pan-hermeneutic cultural anthropologists, in particular.

Surely one of the most ironic consequences of pan-hermeneutic imperialism in the social and cultural sciences and of its strong distinction between the human and natural sciences especially is that, in the course of shielding some dimensions of human affairs from causal explanation, pan-hermeneuts have generally relinquished the natural sciences to traditional logical empiricism. Thus, they have largely presumed the soundness for the natural sciences of logical empiricist accounts of scientific explanation (in terms of deductions from causal laws) and of cross-scientific relations (in terms of intertheoretic "reduction"). Over the past two decades, a huge literature has emerged that not only challenges the appropriateness of these models for the analysis of the *natural* sciences but offers alternative accounts (e.g., Bechtel and Richardson 1993).

The assumptions of antiquated conceptions of cross-scientific relations in terms of intertheoretic *reduction*, which envision the ability of lower level theories to displace higher level proposals and their ontologies, have haunted cultural anthropologists from afar. Much recent work in the philosophy of science would aid considerably in exorcising these demons.

For example, recent philosophical models of cross-scientific relations emphasize the *benefits* that arise for both upper and lower level investigations from multilevel research in science (see especially Wimsatt 1976; Bechtel 1986; P. S. Churchland 1986; McCauley 1986a, 1996). Scientists are not nearly as interested in theoretical and ontological economizing as philosophers have been. Science is too opportunistic an undertaking. When scientists look— either up or down—to research at other levels, their aim is typically to gain theoretical inspiration, to borrow experimental techniques, or to obtain additional evidence to help with unsolved problems at their own level of analysis. Contrary to classical reductionism, displacing work at other levels is usually the last thing on scientists' minds! Little, if any, evidence exists in twentieth-century science of such displacements of theory or ontology arising as the result of investigations simultaneously carried on at multiple levels of analysis (McCauley 1996).

The success of multilevel cooperation in twentieth-century science (consider, for example, the course of research in genetics over the past fifty years) strongly suggests that anthropologists needlessly impoverish their investigations when, insisting on the autonomy of culture and of cultural explanations, they hope to insulate their theoretical proposals from psychological or biological research.

Exploring the implications of psychological models for cultural phenomena will no more eliminate the need for cultural research and modeling than exploring the implications of the double helix for genetics eliminated research and modeling in that field. It will only result in more sophisticated findings all around. (Consider too the cross-fertilization between neuroscientific and psychological accounts of memory and perception over the past two decades. See Gazzaniga 1988; Neisser 1994, respectively.)

Students of culture should look for tactical, theoretical, explanatory, and evidentiary angles wherever they can be found. The goal of cross-scientific explorations is to enhance the methodological refinement, the theoretical penetration, or the empirical accountability of one or more of the sciences involved. Nor must we presume that either the ampliative resources or the corrective influences must always originate at the lower level. Most interlevel forays of these sorts prove *mutually* enriching for the disciplines involved.

Insisting upon investigative isolation rarely abets explanatory progress. Cultural anthropology pays too high a price for its putative autonomy. Autonomy claims make mischief mostly. They have obscurantist consequences, discouraging scholars from exploring related avenues of research at other levels of analysis. Any science allegedly autonomous of other sciences isn't—in one sense or the other. I hope to dissuade those cultural anthropologists who have not relinquished hope for scientific explanations of cultural phenomena not only from resting content with pan-hermeneutics but also from adopting the autonomy of culture thesis. Pan-hermeneutics, among other failings, congratulates anthropologists for subscribing to the autonomy of culture thesis, and that thesis needlessly restricts sources of theoretical inspiration, methodological insight, and evidential support.

The commonplace and the cognitive

I have argued that cultural anthropologists cannot at the same time readily uphold the autonomy of culture, the psychic and cognitive unity of humankind, and the possibility of obtaining *penetrating* explanations of cultural phenomena. Of these three theses I contend that they should abandon the first, since the consequences of adopting it diminishes the interest of the other two.

If that line of argument has been successful, then I have removed one of the existing barriers to the proposal that cognitive findings and methods can illuminate the study of cultural systems and of religious systems in particular. The second barrier is of a more practical sort. It should not be removed so much as scaled. A brief historical overview will help to clarify matters here.

For a large part of this century, scientifically minded anthropologists and scholars of religion could hardly be faulted for neglecting psychology, for most of psychology, arguably, had little to offer those concerned to develop scientific approaches to cultural materials. Clinically inspired works, especially Freud's, supplied and continue to supply abundant conceptual and theoretical resources (patricide, death wishes, etc.) for explaining a huge range of religious phenomena (see, for example, Nuckolls 1993). Still, scholars in religion and anthropology have typically appropriated those resources only within overtly hermeneutic projects (e.g., Obeysekere 1990) or within projects that suffer from many of the same problems that plague Freud's own proposals—at least when they are construed as theoretical explanations in science.

Different critics raise different objections. The two most prominent complaints from the standpoint of those with scientific interests are either that the Freudian proposals are so underspecified and flexible that no empirical finding can defeat them or that where they are well-specified, the empirical findings defeat them overwhelmingly (Popper 1963; Spence 1982; Grunbaum 1984).

Even for the scientifically scrupulous, neither of these objections should disqualify Freudian work from further consideration. That to this day psychoanalytically inspired approaches probably dominate that subfield known as psychological anthropology is testimony to the suggestiveness of Freud's ideas. The point is simply that such proposals have remained sufficiently problematic (either conceptually or empirically) that they have not emerged as the vanguard of a progressive research program within scientific psychology for explaining aspects of either culture or religion.

If scientifically productive commerce between cultural and religious studies and that side of psychology inspired by clinical experience has been unimpressive in the twentieth century, experimental psychology has had even less to offer, at least until the last three decades. For the previous fifty years, behaviorism in one of its forms or another had dominated experimental psychology. No movement in psychology has been less suited to collaborate with the sociocultural sciences.

Repulsed by the vagaries of the introspectionist psychology that dominated at the turn of the century and encouraged by the logical positivists' account of the meanings of scientific terms, which required the semantic reduction of theoretical concepts to exclusively observational foundations, most behaviorists sought either the elimination of standard theoretical concepts—in psychology these are typically mentalistic concepts—or their exhaustive explication in terms of observable behavior. Behavioral psychology, in effect, aimed to purge itself of as much theory as possible, since theoretical claims introduce both vaguenesses and substantive commitments that go well beyond the data. Some behaviorists (e.g., Tolman 1967) argued for the importance of such theoretical notions for the adequate description of behavior and some logical empiricists (e.g., Hempel 1965) recognized that it is precisely such conceptual flexibility and leaps beyond the facts that are the critical contributions of theorizing to scientific progress, but both groups simply proposed greater tolerance and continued to operate within the dominant paradigms of their respective disciplines. More radical critics of both behavioral psychology (such as Chomsky 1959; Brewer 1974) and the underlying philosophy of science (such as Quine 1953; Popper 1959; Kuhn 1970) helped to foment the transformation of these fields over the past thirty years.

Whatever the liabilities that plague psychoanalytic schemes, Freudian ideas have generated a steady stream of explanatory proposals in religion and anthropology. By contrast, behaviorists' begrudging attitudes toward theoretical expansiveness have rendered their *conceptual frameworks* virtually worthless to students of culture. Their *findings* have generally proven no more helpful.

As with any rigorously experimental science, both classical and operant conditioning depend upon experimenters maintaining tight control over extremely simple environments. This usually assures both the replicability and the clarity of results. But as humanists and anthropologists of virtually all stripes have hastened to note, neither human beings nor their everyday environments are so simple or so easy to control. Psychology is unlikely to provide anthropologists or scholars of religion with helpful insights into cultural and religious matters, if its explanatory accomplishments turn so fundamentally on stripping the environment of most of its cultural or religious interest.

Behaviorism's fifty year reign in experimental psychology thoroughly thwarted whatever grip inventive experimentalists might have achieved on such fronts. The simplified environments its investigative methods required served only to obstruct the development of an experimental psychology of religion. Its antitheoretical penchant also impeded the formulation of theories capable of bridging psychological findings and larger cultural patterns. (On this count, even the most tough-minded champions of scientific approaches owe a debt of gratitude to Freud.) Behaviorism's dominance insured that the psychology of religion remained at the extreme periphery of experimental psychology and that general questions about the connections between psychology and culture did not often arise.

An important part of anthropology's business is simply cataloguing the details of diverse cultures. If cultural explanation *is* a possibility, it should come as no surprise that anthropologists would be interested in explanatory theories that identify and connect patterns amid the variability of those details. For a large part of this century, cultural anthropologists and scholars of religion judged *correctly* that the dominant school of experimental psychology offered them few useful resources.

Of course, behaviorism's methodological restrictions were not the only obstacles to experimental work in the psychology of religion. In fact, in experimental psychology's initial decades many important figures, such as Wundt, Galton, and James, had considerable interest in the psychology of religion. But sociocultural systems of this sort have proven among the most difficult beasts science has ever aimed to tame. They do not easily succumb to experimentation, test, or control. The study of such systems presents numerous problems, beginning with the problem of even clarifying what they are. Religions, for example, are not physical things. They are also not spatially localizable. Much about them is not readily observable. They seem ineliminably symbolic. They undergo gradual but constant change. Even at any one point in time they seem to encompass considerable variability in both form and content. Thus, as noted earlier, individuating one from another is no simple task. Religion is people and their practices, their mental states, their actions, their symbols, their communities, their sacred texts, and more. A religious system is always larger than all of its parts, but it also involves individual experience at its core. *That* has always seemed the natural opening for experimental psychology's entry into the study of religion.

Still, obvious problems persist. Religious experiences are not readily elicited in psychological laboratories. The impact of prayer, even on the pray-er, is a difficult thing to judge, let alone measure (Gould 1981: 75). Extended rituals introduce more variables than any psychologist is likely ever to be able to control. For a host of reasons having to do with its character, its eliciting conditions, its special cultural status, and more, religious experience, perhaps more than any other culturally defined experience, does not readily submit to the techniques of psychological experimentation and test. The very nature of the beast poses significant obstacles to rigorous scientific study. Thus, it should come as little surprise that for nearly a hundred years *The Varieties of Religious Experience* remains the single most influential work in the field or that James' approach in that book falls short of the standards that characterize experimental science.

The force of the previous sentence is congratulatory, not dismissive. James conscientiously catalogues the enormous variety of experiences reported in the history of religions—including everything from the extremes of religious asceticism to chloroform-induced mystical states! He examines and evaluates numerous explanatory proposals, and he advances hypotheses of his own, concerning especially the priority of feeling over cognition in religious experience and the close relation of many forms of religious experience to the "transmarginal or subliminal region" of consciousness (1902/1929: 473).

Sorting through the immense collection of materials James surveys has remained the task of subsequent generations of researchers. As we have already noted, most have brought clinically inspired interests and theories to bear on these materials. Throughout the twentieth century, the exploration of religious materials in experimental psychology has remained a largely peripheral enterprise.

Much of the work that has been done, though, retains two features of James' discussion that we suspect has *discouraged* the development and elaboration of psychological hypotheses as a means of gaining insight into religious systems. The first is James' presumption that religious experience is fundamentally affective. James states that

> you suspect that I am planning to defend feeling at the expense of reason, to rehabilitate the primitive and unreflective....
>
> To a certain extent I have to admit that you guess rightly. I do believe that feeling is the deeper source of religion, and that philosophic and theological formulas are secondary products. (1902/1929: 422)

The point is not that these claims are false. (Indeed, Justin Barrett and Frank Keil's [1996] studies suggest that substantial conceptual distance separates most subjects' avowed formal, theological conceptions of God and a much more anthropomorphic conception utilized in their "on-line" reasoning.) Rather the point is that James' focus on the place of emotion in religious experience invites just the sort of reductionistic analyses that cultural anthropologists disdain. Neuroscience has probably made more progress in the explanation of emotion than in any other area of human experience. Not only cultural considerations but psychological ones as well are largely subordinated in neurophysiological analyses of emotional states.

The second feature of James' treatment that has probably inhibited the development of general psychological theories about patterns of religious experience turns on his distinction between original and "second-hand religious life." At the outset of *Varieties* James declares:

> I speak not now of your ordinary religious believer, who follows the conventional observances ... His religion has been made for him by others, communicated to him by tradition, determined to fixed forms by imitation, and retained by habit. *It could profit us little to study this second-hand religious life.* We must make search rather for the original experiences which were the pattern-setters to all this mass of suggested feeling and imitated conduct. (1902/1929: 7–8, emphasis added)

James advocates focusing on the extraordinary over the ordinary, a focus inspired by James' metaphysical interests, but, unfortunately, a focus that raises three closely related problems for psychological research.

First, it deters the collection and analysis of data from populations, which is the most popular and successful research strategy in experimental psychology. It is extremely difficult to gather data about those whose experience is "original" in James' sense. Even if James' distinction between original and second-hand experience can be made out precisely (we suspect that it cannot) and even if it tracks some critical variable (we suspect that it does not), inevitably, much, if not most, of the available data is anecdotal, idiosyncratic, and painfully incomplete (from the standpoint of testing relevant hypotheses).

The second problem results directly from the first. A focus on the details of extreme or unusual or even aberrant cases does not abet either the formulation or the testing of general, widely applicable theoretical principles. Typically, in science the atypical serves as a reservoir of information for evaluating hypotheses about some mechanism's *normal* functioning. (Consider, for example, the place of lesion studies in research on the brain [see P. M. Churchland and P. S. Churchland 1996].) By contrast, James eschews hypothesizing about normal cases. Whatever the interest and appeal of James' catalogue of extraordinary religious sensibilities, it is unclear how generally applicable the findings will prove. If James' suspicions are right that everyday religious experiences are distant, "second-hand" versions of "original" religious experience, then it is also not at all obvious why analyses of the latter should illuminate the former. This is the cost of focusing on the exotic and the extraordinary.

This leads straightaway to a third problem. James seems to hold that most everyday religious experience is but a pale imitation of the originating experiences of the religiously gifted. This may well be, but if it is so, then James himself has provided grounds for skepticism about its relevance to enhanced understanding of conventional patterns of religious behavior, which, *crucially*, constitute the *vast majority* of people's religious experiences. When psychologists of religion adopt James' strategy of studying the varieties of (extraordinary) religious experience, they constantly risk doing so at the cost of studying most of religious experience.

These three concerns jointly suffice to justify considering additional psychological approaches to the study of religion. Our own proposal is to reverse these two emphases in James' work, that is, to examine *cognitive* (as opposed to affective) dimensions of *commonplace* (as opposed to extraordinary) patterns of religious behavior and experience. That said, though, the question still remains as to what form such investigations should take.

Advantages of a competence approach to religious materials

The decisive turn in experimental psychology away *from* behaviorism could be generally characterized as a turn *toward* the construction and evaluation of hypotheses about minds. Minds, however, may not seem any more accessible to systematic study than cultural systems. The most important methodological accomplishment of the cognitive sciences and of the so-called cognitive revolution in experimental psychology is precisely their success in showing ways minds *are* accessible to scientific study. The flourishing of the cognitive sciences over the past two decades has amply illustrated just how models of the mind are empirically (and experimentally) tractable.

But while minds may be easier to study, it remains to be seen whether they are appropriate things to study when the ultimate objects of explanation are cultural phenomena. The argument for that claim comes with the recognition that human minds are the repositories of extensive knowledge about sociocultural systems. This general approach holds that if sociocultural systems, like natural languages or religious systems or systems of etiquette, so resist scientific scrutiny (for the standard reasons having to do with their complexity, scale, amorphousness, diffuseness, and so on), then a good place to look for further evidence about their character is in the minds of individual participants familiar with those systems. If the systems are hard to handle, perhaps, participants' *knowledge* of those systems will prove easier to corral.

If all of the critical knowledge these participants possess were available to them consciously, then only the jobs of collecting it and organizing it theoretically would remain. Many of the pertinent knowledge structures, though, are neither consciously entertained nor consciously accessible. Native speakers of a language, for example, usually have little or no sense of what knowledge structures or cognitive processes inform their facility with the syntax of their language. Their knowledge of such systems is held "tacitly," that is, it is held almost completely unreflectively below the level of consciousness (Chomsky 1972). It is only when we attempt to learn some foreign language that we realize both how complex syntax is and how difficult it is to master when relying heavily on conscious processing.

The overwhelming majority of the time speakers do not consciously aim to speak or write grammatically.[1] They just do it "without thinking." (The same goes for experienced practitioners vis-à-vis their religious rituals.) Nor are speakers typically capable of either pronouncing upon purported grammatical principles or proposing one of their own. Such principles are usually not objects of our conscious, intentional states. Instead, researchers elicit participants' intuitions about particular cases (both real and hypothetical ones) and can use that information to shape their hypotheses about the language's underlying principles.

A central claim of our project is that on most fronts a participant's competence with a religious ritual system constitutes a parallel state of affairs to the linguistic case. Participants in religious ritual systems possess a similar sort of tacit knowledge concerning the constraints on the well formedness of their religious rituals. Like speakers of a language, they have acquired much, if not most, of this knowledge without explicit instruction. Moreover, they have the same sort of intuitive access to normative judgments about such matters, even though they are commonly as unaware of the principles and processes that inform these judgments as speakers are of the grammatical principles that inform their linguistic intuitions.

All of this is to say that both natural languages and religious ritual systems are what Lawson and I (1990: 2–3) have called "symbolic-cultural systems." Both are organized, supra-individual systems of practices and patterns in participants' conduct, utterances, and beliefs about which they are capable of rendering largely similar judgments concerning a huge range of cases and features, even though they are mostly unaware of the bases for those judgments.

The methodological question is how scientists can gain knowledge of these cognitive, even if not-always-conscious, processes and states. The methodological recommendation is that instead of focusing on either the emotional or the extraordinary character of religious experiences, as so many researchers have in the experimental psychology of religion, or opting out of the science business altogether (as so many cultural anthropologists have), scholars concerned with the import of the psychological dimensions of religion should look to the *cognitive* revolution for inspiration.

Specifically, I am suggesting that other sociocultural systems and religious ritual systems, in particular, may fruitfully submit to a competence approach to theorizing at the sub-personal level. The proximal goal of such a theory is to outline a simple, unified system of principles that will account both for the pattern and character of the indefinitely large set of judgments participants can make about the forms of their religious rituals and for the relative uniformity of a vast number of those judgments across informants. The theory's ultimate goal is to explain something of the pattern and character of participants' actual conduct.

Such an approach to religious ritual systems circumvents two features that frequently arise in much research in standard psychology of religion and, as noted in the previous section, that often seem to impede theoretical and empirical progress. There, recall, I noted that ever since James, even psychologists of religion with experimental interests have highlighted (1) emotional rather than cognitive dimensions of religious experience and, frequently, (2) the religious experiences of extraordinary rather than ordinary participants in religious systems.

A competence theory at the sub-personal level takes a very different approach. Proceeding at the sub-personal level, our theory proposes an array of *non*conscious states and processes. Consequently, it offers some relief from worries about doing justice to the experiential nuances of each new manifestation of religiosity. Moreover, our theory of religious ritual competence focuses primarily on cognitive rather than emotional aspects of religious experience. Competence theories seek to explain judgments about the forms of sociocultural events in terms of cognitive structures.

Nor are competence theories plagued by worries of generalizability due to a preoccupation with the extraordinary. Theories of competence aim to describe knowledge held in common by virtually all participants in a symbolic-cultural system. Those theories' ultimate goal is to account for normal functioning within some symbolic-cultural system, consequently, they concentrate on general rather than singular knowledge structures.

A theory of religious ritual competence will contribute to our understanding of religious ritual *behavior*, because the performance of religious ritual, unlike linguistic performance, typically involves the interference of far fewer "irrelevant conditions" than does linguistic performance. The primary reason is that the toleration of variation in religious ritual performance is much less than it is with language use. Consequently, considerations extraneous to religious ritual form are less likely to arise. My argument, then, is not that our current theory of religious ritual competence provides any finer grained account of the actual cognitive representations participants employ, but rather that the "central range" of "stable states of the system" for which a competence theory is "descriptively adequate" will include a much greater proportion of the relevant cases overall. This substantially narrows the gap between religious ritual competence and religious ritual behaviors.

Whether narrowing *that* gap will aid in narrowing the gap between a theory of religious ritual competence and the cognitive processing—associated with religious ritual behaviors is unclear. If it does, though, it will certainly depend upon a continuing coevolution of competence, performance, and processing accounts.

My goal is, precisely, to initiate that coevolution by illustrating how our theory has identified the critical variables that explain several aspects of religious ritual performance. Whether this will justify any strong presumptions about psychological processes or not, it *will* exhibit the sort of productive interplay between a competence theory and considerations of performance and processing that will illuminate elementary forms of religious performance.

Twenty-Five Years In: Landmark Empirical Findings in the Cognitive Science of Religion

Religious Studies' collective advocacy on behalf of diversity and inclusion stands in poignant contrast to its persisting *exclusionary* ethos (within most quarters of the field) concerning questions of method. A legacy of prohibitions in Religious Studies about who can study religions and about how they must proceed when doing so has tended to curb innovation. Born of protectionism (Lawson and McCauley 1990: chapter 1) or special pleading (McCauley 2013) or outright religious impulses (Lawson and McCauley 1993; Martin and Wiebe 2012), such prohibitions have skewed the field in favor of the idiosyncratic over the recurrent, of the idiographic over the systematic, and of the interpretive over the explanatory. My long-standing interest in the promise of the cognitive sciences for studying religion has been, in part, to redress those imbalances. Redressing imbalances, however, does not involve dismissing the idiosyncratic, the idiographic, or the interpretive, but only suggests, first, that they are not the whole story and, second, that greater attention to the recurrent, the systematic, and the explanatory will enrich—not eliminate—our understandings and our inquiries.

The first of those two propositions follows from the second. My aim in this paper, and in this book overall is to substantiate that second proposition. Up to now, I have offered two lines of philosophical argument in its support—one broad and one more narrow, which I briefly summarize in the next two sections. The remaining sections of this chapter advance a further set of considerations in support of the cognitive science of religion (CSR hereafter) based on its many *scientific* successes.

Explanatory pluralism

The first broad line of philosophical argument in defense of my contention that systematic explanations about recurrent patterns in religious systems will enhance our understanding of religious phenomena (developed in Lawson and McCauley 1990; McCauley 2000, 2013; McCauley and Lawson 1996) follows from general positions in the philosophy of science about the character and consequences of cross-scientific relations and their implications for explanations in science (McCauley 1986a, 1996, 2007). CSR and the cognitive sciences generally are but instances of cross-scientific investigations to which these general positions' verdicts apply.

Both CSR and the cognitive sciences, more generally, exemplify the *explanatory pluralism* that prevails in cross-scientific contexts throughout the sciences (McCauley 2013). For new purposes pertaining to their own inquiries, scientists frequently enlist the conceptual, theoretical, analytical, methodological, experimental, and evidential resources developed within other sciences that are pursued at what are, sometimes, quite distant analytical levels. The various cognitive sciences span multiple analytical levels, generating and integrating insights from the biological, psychological, and social sciences—*from* cognitive neuroscience and comparative psychology at the biological level *to* cognitive and cultural anthropology at the sociocultural level *and everything in between.* They have assembled an extensive collection of investigative techniques and developed pictures both of human behavior and of the structure and operations of the human mind that are far more penetrating and insightful than those available heretofore. Their impact has been transformational in linguistics and economics, and they hold comparable potential for the study of politics, for the study of society and culture generally, *and for the study of religion.*

The resulting integrative accounts of religious phenomena in CSR certainly *extend* our understanding of the variety of factors that may be influencing religious thought and action in diverse locales. Those accounts also increase the range of resources available for situating phenomena conceptually and theoretically. Explanatory pluralism highlights the many means by which scientific investigators exploit the varied resources of the sciences and scientists' opportunistic approach to evidence, in particular.

Explicitly aiming in cross-scientific settings to *supplant* prevailing theories and the approaches that inspire them (e.g., Bickle 2003) ignores both the normative and historical considerations that animate explanatory pluralism. In particular, it contravenes scientists' bountiful opportunism regarding evidence. The replacement of theories and approaches that these positions envision would only reduce the number and variety of assets available in cross-scientific inquiries. More important, perhaps, the history of science supplies few, if any, precedents for such aspirations, especially once the pertinent inquiries enjoy some measure of intellectual and institutional stability (McCauley 2007, 2013).

This is *not* to say that the reduction or the elimination of theories in science never occurs. They sometimes do, but the consequences of the first, that is, reduction, and the contexts in which the second, that is, elimination, occur *carry no deleterious implications for the relationship between CSR and conventional Religious Studies*. With regard to the first, the smooth mappings between cognitive theories and interpretive proposals implicated in a scientific reduction serve to *vindicate* the interpretive account in the specific context it addresses. With regard to the second, the replacement, indeed, the outright elimination of theories and their accompanying ontologies is the outcome of intense competition *within* some science over time between clearly incompatible theories (McCauley 1986a, 1996, 2007). Historically, such intense competition between what Thomas Kuhn (1970) called "incommensurable" alternatives tends to be comparatively short-lived (often but a decade or two) in the experimental sciences (Thagard 1992). Concentrated experimental research reveals the new competitor's strengths and liabilities relative to those of the prevailing theory, and either the relevant scientific community eschews the upstart or the field undergoes a scientific revolution that eliminates that previously prevailing theory and at least a few of its ontological commitments.

Crucially, the sorts of *cross-scientific contexts* in which any incompatibilities between cognitive theories and interpretive proposals would arise at some point in time are not, historically, situations that occasion scientific revolutions. Substantial conceptual and theoretical incompatibilities in cross-scientific contexts may generate selection pressures between analytical levels, but the history of science indicates that such inter-level pressures rarely, if ever, suffice to bring about such stark outcomes. No scientific consideration requires such a draconian approach to resolving theoretical incompatibilities *across* analytical levels in science. Instead of these selection pressures pushing in the direction of revolutionary upheaval at some analytical level, they may just as well ignite efforts to forge cross-scientific connections, especially when the research programs in question are pursued within scientific disciplines that have long-standing intellectual and institutional legacies.

The consistent emphasis in CSR on *explicitly* formulating theories in detail is an unqualified virtue. It helps to clarify the points where, whatever their provenance, theoretical proposals may make contact as well as whether points of contact are likely to result in conflicts or connections.

Whether through providing speculative interpretive proposals, or counter-instances that challenge cognitive hypotheses, or recommendations for refining such hypotheses, or focused scrutiny on relevant phenomena, or through simply presenting basic findings to be made sense of, standard work in Religious Studies and the History of Religions can engage in myriad collaborative enterprises with cognitive scientists of religion. Historians' findings about both persisting and extinct religions, in particular, are a test-track on which, sooner or later, cognitive theories must run (Whitehouse and Martin 2004; Pyysiäinen and Uro 2007; Martin and Sørensen 2011; Czachesz and Uro 2013; Martin 2015).

The sorts of findings in CSR that the sections "The Development of CSR ..." to "New Directions" survey as well as those in the cognitive sciences generally offer scholars of religion plentiful resources for inspiring and refining interpretive proposals. The cognitive sciences have collectively uncovered grounds for contextualizing, qualifying, supplementing, and, in some circumstances, even superseding many of the stock assumptions of common-sense psychology that inform interpretive approaches to human mental life, discourse, and action. Presumptions that seeing is believing, that the conscious mind matters most, that the mind's operations can go on in comparative isolation from the body, that memory is retrieval of fixed snapshots of past events, that possessing false memories follows from either some functional impairment or intentional perversity, that we mean what we say, that people have privileged knowledge about the workings of their own minds, and so on must all be hedged in one way or another most of the time. That alone is probably not news to humanists. What the cognitive sciences deliver, though, are increasingly detailed accounts of why and when and how and how much they should be hedged—detailed accounts which have withstood exacting empirical scrutiny and experimental tests.[1]

The cognitive sciences pose no barriers to humanists' interpretive projects. Familiarity with those sciences' accomplishments should abet the sophistication of interpretive proposals (Lawson and McCauley 1990: chapter 1).[2]

Avoiding the quandaries of interpretive exclusivism

The second line of philosophical argument defending CSR's potential to enrich inquiries addressing religious phenomena (developed in Lawson and McCauley 1993 and McCauley 2000) concerns its abilities to supply constructive responses to moral, epistemic, and metaphysical quandaries that other prominent approaches in the study of religion face. These include crises of conscience, riddles of identity, epistemic over-confidence, and metaphysical muddles.

E. Thomas Lawson and I (1993) pointed to the crisis of conscience in anthropology and to the inadequacies of interpretive methods for addressing it. In the subsequent two decades, scholars' moral sensitivities have appropriately expanded beyond questions of colonialism to include persisting forms of oppression of women, people of color, people of various racial, ethnic, and religious backgrounds as well as the poor, the disabled, and people with any of a variety of sexual and gender identities (who do not benefit from heterosexual privilege as a result), *wherever* they may reside. These forms of oppression no less merit our moral concern, but they are no better confronted by antiscientific ideology than was colonialism in the mid- and late twentieth century.

Antiscientific enthusiasts' claims, first, that with scientific knowledge comes power to oppress and, second, that the interests of oppressors and scientists often coincide are both surely true. But stopping there neglects the further truth that no human undertaking and, certainly, no human undertaking on the scale that modern science is pursued comes close to the level of self-policing that science achieves. Of course, that self-policing pertains most directly to epistemic rather than moral matters,[3] but, crucially, to the extent that scientific rationality and morality both turn on ideals about honesty and truth (however the latter should be characterized), they are of a piece. Its self-policing helps to ensure that science is unsurpassed as a tool for obtaining knowledge about the world of our experience and that, barring its obliteration (a fairly high price to pay for oppressors who putatively rely on science as a means to power), its verdicts are neither wholly nor finally subordinate to the powerful. Antiscientific enthusiasts' suggestions—that the best response to the use of science to oppress is to abandon science and its ideals—are counterproductive. For example, the cognitive sciences can aid us, not least, in gaining a deeper understanding of human moral psychology (e.g., Graham et al. 2013).

Over the last few decades scholars of religion have recognized that, to the extent that the field of Religious Studies has itself collaborated with cultural anthropology and pursued parallel projects, it has been something of an unindicted co-conspirator in these crises of conscience. Lawson and I argue, though, that Religious Studies has an additional problem concerning its identity as an intellectual project. Long wary of being categorized with either theology or the social sciences, Religious Studies programs have mostly sought a haven within the humanities. Traditionally, the principal defense for that position has maintained that Religious Studies has either a unique object of study, a unique method for studying that object, or both. Those assumptions, however, have undergone withering criticism from multiple quarters—not only from cognitive scientists of religion. Arguments about the exclusivity of religious materials and the methods for their study have faced at least two major objections.

The first objection concerns the very notion that distinctively *religious* materials even exist. Cognitive scientists of religion and many recent contributors to Religious Studies question the viability of "religion" as an analytical category and its (metaphysical) status as an object of study. Although their reasons for skepticism that "religion" designates a unified body of phenomena differ, they are consistent and complementary grounds for that negative conclusion.

The by-product theory is the earliest and remains the most prominent theoretical orientation in the cognitive science of religion (Guthrie 1980, 1993; Lawson and McCauley 1990; Whitehouse 1992, 1995; Boyer 1994, 2001; McCauley and Lawson 2002). The by-product theory holds that religions, like various other cultural arrangements from folklore to militaries, engage a host of ordinary cognitive systems (theory of mind, contamination avoidance, kinship recognition, linguistic competence, etc.) that are in place on the basis of considerations that have nothing to do with one another and, crucially for current purposes, considerations that have *nothing to do with religion*. Those cognitive capacities' exercise in religious contexts results in by-products of their normal functioning. Whether they concern anthropomorphism (Guthrie 1993), action representation (Lawson and McCauley 1990), episodic and autobiographical memory (Whitehouse 2004), or all of these and more (Boyer 2001), these cognitive capacities exist in human minds because they enable people to deal with the species' perennial problems. It follows that, at least from a cognitive perspective, neither religion nor religiosity is some stable, uniform sensibility or pattern of behavior.

Some dissidents in Religious Studies raise a different set of considerations for questioning the analytical purchasing power of talk about religion. They argue that 'religion' is a concept born of the scholarly enterprise of the modern Western world. The dissidents (e.g., Fitzgerald 2000) note that the concept is tarnished by virtue of its association with the crises of conscience. "Religion" is an analytical term deployed by scholars in the West in an area of study that bolsters the projects of colonialists and capitalists, let alone the projects of proselytizers.

Their complaints, however, are not only moral. The sorts of features that receive scholars' attention favor the arrangements of the religions of the book, primarily, and of the world religions, secondarily, without attention to the understandings, practices, contexts, and lives of the members of the myriad small-scale societies around the world and throughout human history. Dissidents point out that the concept of religion does not seem to exist in many cultures; nor, they note, is there a similar word in many languages. It is precisely the plethora of *apparently* relevant stories, beliefs, actions, practices, social arrangements, institutions, and more as well as the variety of ways that they are regarded from one setting to the next that foil scholars' interminable attempts even to define "religion" (Saler 2008).

From this point, the argument is straightforward. Dissidents regard the lack of consensus among scholars and their persistent failure to define the field and its primary object of study as grounds for the analytical vacuity of the concept 'religion.' Without any defensible, coherent grounds for identifying what should count as religion, the traditional proposal that 'religion' and its cognates pick out exceptional phenomena, whose study requires exceptional methods, seems forlorn.

Casting the discussions at the level of *particular religions*, in order to circumvent the problems associated with religion construed as some general domain of human thought and endeavor, introduces its own metaphysical complexities (McCauley 2000). What kinds of things are religions? Where, exactly, do they exist? How are their boundaries determined? What is the basis of their continuities over time? What, if anything, whether beliefs, practices, or heritages is essential? Who counts as a Muslim or a Christian or a Buddhist and, more important, *who gets to decide*? The latter two questions have acquired considerable poignancy in a time when religiously motivated assaults routinely seize headlines throughout the world, yielding never-ending arguments about who should count as a *true* X, where "X" designates the name of some particular religious affiliation or other. Such talk about who is a "true" X (a true Muslim, a true Christian, etc.) or what makes for "true" X (true Islam, true Christianity, etc.) is transparently normative and that normativity is transparently theological. That leads straightforwardly enough to the second objection.

The second objection to the traditional claims about the unique character of religious materials and the necessity of extraordinary methods for their study holds that the positive case made in their behalf faces a dilemma. Either the arguments commit the fallacy of *petitio principii* (i.e., they assume what they set out to defend) or they depend upon what are, finally, fundamentally theological conceptions of religious matters, with repeated references to "the holy," "the sacred," "the transcendent," and so on. As a way around this dilemma, many scholars recruited broader (but, in most regards, parallel) arguments deployed across the humanities typically about the singular character either of (human) subjectivity (e.g., Nagel 1974) or of the meaningful (e.g., Geertz 1973) or of both. These considerations were alleged, on the positive side, to require phenomenological and hermeneutic methods and, on the negative side, to constitute a barrier to scientific approaches. Without reviewing the academic culture wars of the past fifty years, let it suffice here to make four observations.

First, hermeneuticists' (and their postmodernist offspring's) preoccupations with *the text* and with its interpretation as the dominant metaphor for conceptualizing all meaningful materials—so that, for example, religion in all of its facets is construed as textual—leaves scholars not with matchless methods but with woefully deficient ones. That is because, whatever religion is, it is both much more and much less than texts.[4] This seems transparent with regard both to the ancestry of religion in the prehistory of our species and to what appears to be religious goings-on among nonliterate groups. But that is not the end of it. The myriad activities, items, and settings, let alone the mental states, experiences, and utterances that do not even remotely resemble texts but that play such vital roles in people's lives, in nonliterate *and in literate societies*, operate far beyond the borders of the hermeneuticists' textual spotlight.

An emphasis on the textual also inspires a particular view of the past. History, on this view, is textually based. History is concerned with the production of texts that get to their interpretations of past events and agents primarily through reflections about texts—whether previous texts about those events and agents or texts that those agents produced themselves. With such an approach, the cultural traditions, the salient events, and the past lives of the nonliterate risk *invisibility*. In a scholarly sphere in which both human origins and countless human groups are, in effect, invisible, the religions of large-scale, literate societies and their textually documented traditions inevitably hog the attention. The imbalanced distribution of scholarly attention goes largely unnoticed, because, quite literally, the non-textual is mostly nowhere to be seen.

Second, it is worth noting that even if the positive conclusions about the special status of the subjective and the meaningful are sound, they render *religious* subjectivity and *religious* meaning nothing but subcategories of far more sweeping considerations concerning humanistic pursuits overall. They provide no case (that does not circle back to covert theology) for picking the religious varieties out for special disciplinary treatment. The humanists who champion the subjective and the meaningful have far more ambitious aims than merely insulating religion. They intend to safeguard the researches of *all* of the humanities.

Third, the negative conclusions about the inabilities of the sciences to address such matters is an overreaction to a form of scientific exclusivism (scientism) and a conception of the sciences (logical empiricism) that the cognitive sciences and their practitioners neither endorse nor exemplify. The rejection of unsatisfactory accounts of science and of its reach does not require the rejection of science generally, or of the cognitive sciences, or of CSR.

Fourth, as I noted at the outset, such an exclusionary ethos is ill-advised, because the cognitive sciences and CSR offer invaluable methods and findings for enhancing our understandings both of aspects of subjectivity and of the making, having, and using of meaning in human life in general and in religious contexts in particular. In the absence of compelling arguments for interpretive exclusivism or impenetrable subjectivity and in the face of the myriad successes of the cognitive sciences and of CSR, assertions about science's putative inability to further illuminate these matters begin to look like reactionary protectionism of a field, instead of profound insights about either human life or the limits of scientific inquiry.

In the sections that remain, I will situate and summarize some of those successes of CSR, that is, new theoretical proposals, durable, replicated findings, and promising results in that field. The best evidence for the usefulness of these cognitive scientists' methods is the resilience and the fruitfulness of the ensuing research. A fair sample of the numerous methods that CSR has employed will emerge in the course of reporting on this research. Its explanatory pluralism will be transparent.

The development of CSR as a scientific enterprise with new experimental findings generating theories from the bottom-up

CSR arose from a range of theoretical proposals (Guthrie 1980, 1993; Lawson and McCauley 1990; Whitehouse 1992, 1995; Boyer 1994, 2001; McCauley and Lawson 2002) that share at least three assumptions:

(1) that employing the theories, methods, and findings of the cognitive sciences to study religious thought and behavior would yield valuable new insights,

(2) that the mind has no department of religion, that is, that the mind has no systems, structures, or processes specifically dedicated to managing religious materials, and

(3) that many forms of religious cognition are by-products of the operations of cognitive systems that are in place for reasons having nothing to do either with one another or with how they figure in religious matters.

Consistent with the second and third assumptions, these various theoretical works address a wide variety of religious matters and a comparable array of cognitive functions and systems.

CSR began very much as a top-down endeavor. To their credit theoreticians both welcomed attempts to test their hypotheses and explored relevant empirical evidence themselves (Boyer and Walker 2000; McCauley and Lawson 2002; Whitehouse and Laidlaw 2004; Whitehouse and Martin 2004; Whitehouse and McCauley 2005). They also worked to bring empirical evidence to bear on the *comparisons* of theories (e.g., McCauley and Lawson 2002). In doing so, they demonstrated that the research enterprise in which those theories figured qualified as *empirical science*. Still, most of this work involved appeals to ethnographies, case studies, and historical illustrations, which, because of their particularity, disclose only thin slices of the vast landscape of phenomena that pertain to the assessment of any particular theory and, because of origins independent of the theories in question, fail to illuminate many of the parts of that landscape that are of greatest interest. The original theoreticians saw that in addition to simply marshaling available empirical evidence, CSR would clearly benefit from taking the additional step of becoming an *experimental science* (Barrett and Lawson 2001; Boyer and Ramble 2001; Atkinson and Whitehouse 2010).

Experiments not only *test* theories, they *produce* (new) empirical evidence. Testing theories experimentally helps to guard against the biases that may influence theoretical partisans' selections among already available, less systematic, empirical evidence that they cite in support of their theories. Experimentation enables scientists to target precisely those "parts of that landscape that are of greatest interest." The process of managing unexpected experimental results theoretically may not prevent confirmation bias in scientists, but it does tend to make it more conspicuous when it arises (McCauley 2011).

Speculative theoretical ventures like CSR eventually require the kind of systematic support from the bottom-up that elaborate programs of experimentation furnish. Scientific theories should not only be able to fly. They should also be able to land. When theoreticians assemble existing evidence, they are, in effect, carefully selecting spots, surveyed from above, to bring their theoretical aircraft in for a landing. By noting this, I do not intend to be dismissive. Touching down on the hard surfaces of the facts like that *is* an accomplishment; however, experimentation forces theories to the ground at points of interest to those who are watching from below and negotiating conditions there. The more points on the map (i.e., the more facts designated by experimentation) where a theory can land safely, the more worthy it is.

Their common assumptions notwithstanding, these early theories in CSR have never been fully integrated. Still, as research has proceeded, these theoretical proposals have been expounded in ways that have revealed plentiful points of contact and coincidences of views. What, finally, is of far greater usefulness, though, are their conflicts and disagreements both with one another and with other theories that have been proposed subsequently (e.g., Bering 2006), for they serve as invitations to experimentalists to explore competing theories' implications in unusual settings that allow for the control of the theoretically interesting variables.

As noted, CSR began as a high-level, theoretical project. Over the subsequent twenty-five years many of the associated programs of research have secured their credentials not only as empirical science but, in many cases, as experimental science as well.[5] Once experimentation commences in any science, it exhibits a dynamic of its own. Initial findings from experiments aimed at testing big theories inevitably spawn dozens of finer-grained hypotheses. Those hypotheses address what the experiments' findings hint about potentially relevant variables. Reliably, some of those phenomena prove to be, simultaneously, so complex and so theoretically suggestive that they become objects of sustained investigation on their own.

Within CSR various topics are receiving such on-going experimental investigation. These include such effects as theological incorrectness, promiscuous teleology, and characteristic patterns of reasoning about dead agents' minds as well as the mnemonic effects of minimally counter-intuitive representations and the consequences of ritual for building social cohesion and increasing cooperation within groups. (See below the fourth, fifth, and sixth sections, respectively.) Beyond the sheer number of experimental papers that have appeared, perhaps the best evidence over the past fifteen years of CSR's status as a maturing experimental science is the emergence of such topics within its purview that have inspired this sort of prolonged and focused experimental scrutiny that takes on a life of its own. For more than a decade, in each case these topics have attracted the attention of several groups of researchers from around the world, who have examined their various facets in considerable detail.

Further evidence of abundant fertile experimental research in CSR is the development of new theories built from the bottom-up. Possessing a collection of robust experimental results that appear to be disparate is what typically leads to constructing theories in such a fashion. Theoretically minded experimentalists propose a non-obvious principle underlying the apparent incongruities among the findings as a means of integrating them theoretically (McCauley and Lawson 1998).

The parade case from recent work in CSR is the cognitive resource depletion theory (Schjoedt et al. 2013). That theory proposes a unified treatment of the cognitive mechanisms undergirding religious ritual. It groups three apparently disparate phenomena pertaining to ritual:

(1) the persistent occurrence for participants in rituals of goal-demotion and causal opacity (Boyer and Liénard 2006; Liénard and Boyer 2006; Nielbo and Sørensen 2011),

(2) the negative effect on memory of the requirement, especially in high-arousal rituals, that participants suppress their emotional responses (Morinis 1985; Xygalatas et al. 2013b), and

(3) the deference participants show to charismatic ritual authorities about the performance and understanding of the rituals in question (Schjoedt et al. 2011).

The theorists argue that each of these patterns involves the depletion of the cognitive resources that participants can bring to performing, remembering, and interpreting rituals. They maintain that, whether by swamping or by starving the relevant cognitive systems' processors during ritual performances, the resulting deprivations of processing resources create opportunities for religious authorities to proffer accounts, either before or after the rituals' performances, about what is transpiring. The theory proposes, in effect, that if people are daunted by mastering causally opaque details in their ritual actions or by controlling themselves in the face of profoundly stimulating sensory pageantry and community engagement or by the expertise of a charismatic ritual officiant, they have little time or energy for encoding ritual details or pondering ritual meanings. The cognitive resource depletion theory readily squares with the supposition that religious ritual systems have evolved to exploit these cognitive vulnerabilities. Such arrangements are likely to reduce the variability in these rites, which creates a space for cultural authorities to prescribe and regularize their performances and interpretations.

Three effects

Basic empirical outcomes sometimes, all by themselves, elicit extended "normal" scientific treatment (Kuhn 1970). Conditional reasoning, flashbulb memory, the false belief task, and change blindness are examples in mainstream cognitive science from the past few decades. Such continued research on these and other phenomena within the cognitive and psychological sciences is part of the reason why Robert Cummins (2000) has stressed that the psychological sciences' principal accomplishments are the discovery of *effects* (the von Restorff Effect [von Restorff 1933], the Stroop Effect [Stroop 1935], the phoneme restoration effect [Warren 1970], the SNARC effect [Dehaene and Mehler 1992], etc.), rather than the formulation of laws.

CSR offers illustrations of Cummins' (2000) observation that the sciences of the mind specialize in the discovery and articulation of effects. Effects are patterns in human performance that are pervasive, but about which, people are often inattentive, if not unconscious. Effects supply insights about how human minds work. For example, the Spacing Effect (e.g., Madigan 1969) is the finding that distributed practice with materials increases the probability of their long-term retention in memory more than the same amount of massed practice does. If occasions for rehearsal are spaced out over time, memory performance is likely to exceed that from employing some small number of massed practice sessions of comparable duration.

Effects also inspire extensive programs of experimental research.

Theological incorrectness

Perhaps the best known effect arising from experimental research in CSR is the proclivity for theological incorrectness. Recondite theological formulations routinely feature counter-intuitive representations. Their counter-intuitiveness, however, is profuse, not minimal. The theologically correct Christian God, for example, is all-good, all-seeing, all-knowing, all-powerful, and all-present. The theologically informed religiosity of educated participants in large-scale, literate societies regularly employs representations that are nearly, if not equally, as *radically* counter-intuitive as the representations scientific theories employ (McCauley 2011).

Carefully formulated, theologically correct texts commonly issue from years of contestation and debate. Scholars may overplay their prominence, at least with regard to their influence on participants' religious understandings and inferential predilections. Justin Barrett and Frank Keil (1996; Barrett 1998) furnish evidence that in on-line tasks, such as processing and recalling narratives, religious people overwhelmingly utilize conceptions driven by the implicit assumptions associated with various unconscious, task-specific systems that appear to underlie so much of popular religious cognition. They designed short narratives about interactions between people and God to be consistent with the theologically correct doctrines, which their experimental participants affirmed when they were directly queried about their beliefs. The participants offered up conventional, theologically correct, non-anthropomorphic conceptions of God that constitute the orthodox beliefs of their doctrinal religious systems. Instead of deploying those theologically complex, ecclesiastically approved, and policed concepts, which they endorsed when questioned directly, Barrett and Keil's experimental participants frequently revert to spontaneous, *theologically incorrect* conceptions in their recollections of these narratives. Participants reason about God on-the-fly similarly to how they reason about Superman. Of course, Superman is an extraordinary character too. But being stronger than a locomotive, moving faster than a speeding bullet, leaping tall buildings in a single bound, and having X-ray vision still falls a good deal short of omnipotence, omnipresence, and omniscience. Barrett and Keil obtained the same findings when the task is merely to paraphrase, rather than recall, the narratives—*even when participants have full access to the texts* they are paraphrasing throughout the task! They obtained such findings with Christians and Jews in America and with Hindus in India. Jason Slone (2004) outlined multiple lines of evidence for similar patterns in additional religions.) Religious participants explicitly affirm theologically correct propositions; they often memorize theologically approved doctrines and learn a good deal of theology themselves (Peterson 2013), but it does not follow that any of this substantially influences how they think and reason *on-line* about religious matters in ordinary settings.

Emma Cohen in her ethnography (2007) and in her experimental work with Barrett (2008a, b) marshals evidence indicating that theological incorrectness occurs even in unpretentious settings in which scholarly sophistication and ecclesiastical hierarchy are meager. They show that theologically incorrect ideas readily intrude in the thought of followers of a small Brazilian spirit-possession cult. In order to handle a variety of theological complications, such as a possessing spirit showing strikingly different personality traits when possessing different people at different times, the cult leader teaches that spirit possession involves the *fusion* of the possessing spirit with the mind of the host. Spirit fusion, however, neither squares with folk psychology nor delivers much inferential potential. It is a substantially counter-intuitive notion that does not comport very well with theory of mind. Cohen found that participants in the spirit-possession cult (and she and Barrett found that experimental participants in other cultures) virtually unanimously opted for the intuitive view (regularly portrayed in Hollywood movies) that the possessing spirit *displaces* the host's spirit, instead. Interestingly, people seem less troubled by the complications that accompany this view, such as what the host's spirit is up to and where it resides when it has been displaced.

The automatic intrusion of these maturationally natural intuitive mental systems guarantees the repeated eruption of theological incorrectness, no matter how humble the religious system. These are instances of a general pattern in which recurring intuitive assumptions connected with basement level cognitive systems intrude in thought and can trump painstakingly acquired reflective knowledge, whether theological or scientific (McCauley 2011).

Promiscuous teleology

A second seminal finding in CSR, which has also sustained an ongoing program of research, concerns an effect that Deborah Kelemen (1999a) has dubbed "promiscuous teleology." Kelemen first carried out experimental studies (1999a, b) supporting the position that children find function, purpose, and design throughout the natural world. She documented preschool age children's inclination to over-attribute functions to things as a result of their new facility with theory of mind and growing experience with purposeful agents pursuing goal-directed actions. Unlike educated American adults, most children this age are willing to attribute functions to entire organisms (e.g., tigers) as well as to natural objects (e.g., icebergs), their parts (e.g., a mountain protuberance), and their properties (e.g., the pointiness of rocks).

In subsequent research, Kelemen and her colleagues have produced grounds for suspecting that the penchant for promiscuous teleology may extend beyond childhood. In experiments with Romani adults, Krista Casler and Kelemen (2008) provide evidence *against* the assumption that the discontinuities between children's teleological promiscuousness and adults' apparent abstemiousness are the inevitable outcomes of development. Like the children Kelemen has studied, uneducated Romani adults differ significantly from educated Romani adults and from educated American adults in their willingness to approve teleological explanations for natural objects.

Education matters, but does it suffice to extinguish promiscuous teleology? Kelemen and Evelyn Rosset (2009) obtained experimental evidence indicating that, at least under some conditions, it does not. They had educated participants, who had, on average, completed 2.5 college level science classes, assess the worthiness of proposed explanations for a range of natural phenomena. Participants who were forced to do the task fast (they had 3.2 seconds to read and respond to each item) proved significantly more likely to endorse incorrect teleological explanations than those not under such time pressures. They did so, even though the speeded conditions had *no effect* on those participants' accuracy with regard to control items. They also found that similar percentages of participants assented to some unwarranted teleological explanations (e.g., "the earth has an ozone layer to protect it from UV light" p. 140) in *all* conditions, time-pressured *or not*. An additional study revealed that educated adults with some experience of college level science appear to think that "natural phenomena exist to benefit each other ..." and are "intrinsically directed towards survival ... and maintaining the Earth's natural equilibrium" (p. 141). Crucially, they did *not* restrict such judgments to biological phenomena. Kelemen et al. (2013) found a similar proclivity for teleological explanation of non-biological natural phenomena in experienced, Ph.D. level, physical scientists with appointments at major American research universities, when they too had to make time-pressured assessments of explanations.

Assembling evidence from a wide array of developmental research in addition to that for children's teleological promiscuousness, Kelemen (2004: 295) has proposed that they are "intuitive theists," that is, that they are naturally inclined to regard natural objects as "nonhuman artifacts" that reflect "nonhuman design." She argues that by school age children possess the requisite mental capacities for thinking about intangible agents,[6] their mental states and design intentions, and the (possible) role of the latter in determining objects' purposes. She notes that the view squares with Margaret Evans' (2000, 2001) findings that up to the age of ten children prefer "creationist" explanations of natural objects, regardless of their upbringing or of their parents' views about religion. It also comports with Barrett's arguments that young children's difficulties with the possibility of others having false beliefs, ironically, indicates that they are better equipped to understand infallible minds than they are the minds of humans (Barrett et al. 2001; Barrett 2012). Presumably, Kelemen's subsequent research on promiscuous teleology in adults (outlined above) adds to the plausibility of her suggestion (2004: 299) that adults, at least in their own less cautious ruminations, are also inclined to presume design intentionally imposed on things throughout their natural surroundings.

Dead agents' minds

Jesse Bering and David Bjorklund (2004) produced a body of findings that points to a third, hitherto unnamed effect concerning human reasoning about dead agents' minds that point to intuitive presumptions about minds outliving bodies. They first demonstrated what might be dubbed the "Dead Agents' Minds Effect" in preschoolers and kindergarteners. Although these young children held discontinuity views about biological functions concerning a dead mouse (e.g., they did not think that the mouse would ever need to go to the bathroom again), large majorities spurned such discontinuities with regard to the mouse's psychobiological or cognitive states. Substantial majorities of these young children thought that the mouse was still hungry (as he was when he died) and that he still wanted to go home (as he was attempting when he met his end).

It is not until late elementary school age that clear majorities of Bering and Bjorklund's participants affirmed discontinuity views about the psychobiological and cognitive states of dead agents' minds. This group was, however, the only group in this study that showed a significant difference in their responses to these two question types. Significantly more late-elementary-school-age children certified discontinuities about psychobiological states than did so with regard to the cognitive states of dead agents' minds.

Bering and Bjorklund's work parallels Kelemen's proposal about intuitive theism in at least two important respects. First, they supplied evidence that children's inclinations toward continuity views about dead agents' minds, although probably enhanced by religious indoctrination, did not depend upon it (Bering et al. 2005). Second, what, initially, looked like a pattern among youngsters proved, upon further experimental investigation, to be manifest in adults as well.

In a further experiment, Bering and Bjorklund examined participants' views about post-mortem organismic and mental states at a much finer grain than in their earlier studies, and they did so not only with kindergarteners and late-elementary-school-age children but also with college-age adults. In this experiment, Bering and Bjorklund posed multiple questions about biological states (e.g., "Do you think that Baby Mouse will ever need to *drink water* again?"), psychobiological states (e.g., "Do you think that Baby Mouse is still *hungry*?"), perceptual states (e.g., "Do you think that Baby Mouse can *see* where he is now?"), desires (e.g., "Do you think that Baby Mouse still *wants* to go home?"), emotional states (e.g., "Do you think that Baby Mouse is still *sad* because he can't find his way home?"), and epistemic states (e.g., "Do you think that Baby Mouse *knows* that he's not alive?"). This experiment basically replicated the findings of Bering and Bjorklund's earlier experiments with the kindergarteners and the late-elementary-school-age children.

The pivotal findings of the experiment, though, concerned the adults' responses. First, like the late-elementary-school-age children, the adults were significantly more likely than the kindergarteners to support discontinuity views with regard to the biological, psychobiological, perceptual, and emotional states as well as with regard to desires. This was *not* true, though, with regard to the mouse's epistemic states. Second, again like the late-elementary-school-age children, the adults were significantly more likely than the kindergarteners to be *consistent* discontinuity theorists, that is, to give discontinuity responses to *every* question of a particular type.

Their findings with their adult participants provided evidence for two conclusions. First, discontinuity views about the organismic and mental states of dead agents would appear to be *learned*, as is, presumably, the view that death involves the *extinction* of the mind, from which such discontinuity views follow. Bering and Bjorklund found a significant effect for age group with regard to discontinuity responses. Late-elementary-school-age children gave more discontinuity responses than kindergarteners and adults gave more still and both differed significantly from the kindergarteners on this front.

Second, although large numbers of adults explicitly avowed extinctionist views about dead agents' minds, many did not seem to subscribe to that view when making judgments about the possibilities pertaining to the more purely psychological states of dead agents' minds. Only half of the adults were consistent discontinuity theorists with regard to epistemic states, in particular. Subsequent research has shown that what is, in effect, religious priming, can amplify such effects (Harris and Gimenéz 2005; Astuti and Harris 2008). K. Mitch Hodge (2011) argues that both Bering and Bjorklund's findings as well as these priming effects depend, more fundamentally, on humans' abilities to carry out off-line social reasoning about absent agents.

Minimally counter-intuitive religious representations

Pascal Boyer's (1994, 2001) account of the cognitive bases of religious representations has inspired several studies exploring his contention that religions' minimally counter-intuitive representations enjoy a mnemonic advantage over unproblematic, intuitive representations (no matter how strange or unusual) and over substantially counter-intuitive representations.[7]

The diversity of religious representations can seem overwhelming. Boyer argues, however, that they are significantly constrained. Humans' unconscious inferences about "intuitive ontology" (2001) figure centrally in Boyer's explanation. Intuitive ontologies constitute foundational theories about kinds of things in the world.

Boyer maintains that religious ontologies follow a standard pattern. Religious concepts violate expectations associated with some member of a small set of intuitive ontological categories, *while preserving* all of that category's further default inferences. That set consists of ANIMAL, PERSON, TOOL, NATURAL OBJECT, and PLANT. Violations of physical, biological, or psychological properties yield concepts with *counter-intuitive* properties, exemplified by walking on water, immortality, and *knowing* other peoples' thoughts, respectively. Those violations are of two sorts. *Breaches* occur when something transgresses a principle of folk-physics, folk-biology, or folk-psychology that ordinarily applies. A person who passes through walls violates intuitive physics. A person who is the offspring of a lion breaches our folk-biological expectations. *Transfers* occur when properties are assigned to items that do not possess them. Talk about a mountain that is alive transfers a collection of biological properties to a natural object. Claims about a snake that talks transfer a collection of sophisticated psychological capacities to an organism without them. Usually these representations involve only one violation in each instance; thus, they are *minimally* counter-intuitive (MCI).[8]

Boyer hypothesizes that MCI concepts enjoy an advantage from the standpoint of competition for humans' attentions, as they approximate a cognitive optimum. First, *all* counter-intuitive concepts are *attention grabbing.* Counter-intuitiveness is not the only way to get noticed, but it suffices. Second, MCI concepts retain substantial *inferential potential.* An MCI concept's single violation leaves its abundant inferential power basically intact. Moses may have parted the Red Sea, but we can still infer that he would have made a splash had he jumped in, that his heart was beating throughout the episode, and that he would have expected that the subsequent inundation of the Egyptians would interrupt their pursuit. These are but three unsurprising inferences, which follow from this story that contains the concept PERSON WHO PARTED THE RED SEA. Boyer accentuates the instantaneousness and alacrity with which humans carry out such inferences and the wealth of inferences available.

The *memorability* of MCI concepts is a third consideration contributing to their selective advantage. MCI concepts not only fascinate, they tend to stick, which is necessary for their transmission. Various experimentalists have tested this hypothesis about MCI concepts' mnemonic advantages. Early studies obtained the predicted effects (Barrett and Nyhof 2001; Boyer and Ramble 2001). In assorted cultural and religious settings on four continents, MCI concepts were remembered significantly better than

- normal, intuitive concepts (e.g., a person who delivers thoughtful sermons and sleeps at night),
- highly unusual but not counter-intuitive concepts (e.g., a chocolate table), and
- substantially counter-intuitive concepts that involve many violations of intuitive assumptions (e.g., a statue that hears and answers prayers, weeps and bleeds, and flies around at night).[9]

Researchers have examined what role other variables may play in facilitating the recollection of MCI concepts. Those variables include imagery (Slone et al. 2007), causal integration (Harmon-Vukić and Slone 2009), background knowledge and narrative context (Gonce et al. 2006; Upal et al. 2007), and the amount of cognitive processing the concept demands (Harmon-Vukić et al. 2012). In each case, the mnemonic advantage accruing to MCI concepts generally stands. Moreover, in these and other studies (e.g., Norenzayan et al. 2006) that advantage increases as retention intervals increase. This was especially true with retention intervals measured in months, which would seem to be the time frames most relevant to matters of cultural transmission (Barrett and Nyhof 2001). Recent experiments indicate that the heightened memorability of MCI concepts holds for children as young as seven (Banerjee et al. 2013).

Occasionally religious representations incorporate more than one violation of humans' ontological intuitions. Moses, for example, has a conversation with a burning bush that is not consumed. Thus, I have suggested that "MCI" might be better construed as *modestly* counter-intuitive (McCauley 2011). Konika Banerjee and her colleagues (2013), in fact, have provided experimental evidence that suggests that the mnemonic advantage for counter-intuitive concepts extends to two violations. They found that seven- to nine-year-old children showed significantly better recall both directly and after one week for concepts involving either one *or two*, but not three, violations of intuitive ontology, relative to intuitive concepts.

New directions

Like cognitive science more generally, CSR has expanded in a variety of new directions in the twenty-first century. The field has attracted greater numbers of researchers, and those researchers have simultaneously advanced new theoretical proposals and introduced many new ways to test them. They have enlisted methods from across the social, cognitive, and brain sciences. The following three subsections will briefly discuss empirical research that simultaneously exhibits: (a) three of these new methods (economic games, brain imaging, and physiological measures in the field) and (b) three of the most conspicuous new directions for research in CSR (evolutionary theorizing, cognitive neuroscience, and religious experience).

These three new directions for research are by no means unique to CSR. They echo research trends across the cognitive sciences.

Evolutionary theorizing

The many controversies they have provoked notwithstanding, the emergence of (1) sociobiology (Wilson 1975), (2) theories of cultural evolution (Boyd and Richerson 1985; Richerson and Boyd 2006; Henrich 2016), and (3) evolutionary psychology (Barkow et al. 1992; Buss 2005) has reintroduced reflection on the evolutionary foundations of cognition and mental life that had, for various reasons, been largely moribund for more than seventy years. Because it connected so directly with an existing experimental paradigm of long-standing interest, viz., the Wason selection task (1966, 1968), Leda Cosmides' (1989) discoveries about the crucial influence of social exchange on conditional inference in that task and the voluminous literature that it subsequently spawned thrust evolutionary considerations into cognitive science. The productive research programs associated with the alliance between evolutionary psychology (Barrett 2015) and cultural group selection and cultural evolution (Henrich 2016) ensure they will not be going away.

It is probably not a coincidence that all of the first generation contributors in CSR were by-product theorists. Among that group, it was Boyer (1994, 2001) who developed what was the most elaborate evolutionary account of religious cognition. Evolutionary psychologists' commitments to the domain specificity of numerous cognitive systems, especially, have informed Boyer's proposals about religious cognition from the outset. Subsequent researchers (such as Bulbulia 2004; Bering 2006) have wedded their views of religious cognition more directly to natural selection, arguing on a variety of grounds that humans' have religious cognitive proclivities because those proclivities are individually adaptive. They maintain that religious sensibilities have aided individuals in passing on their genes.

Those hypotheses typically move in either or both of two directions. The first stresses the beneficial impact of religious participation on human health and well-being (e.g., Bulbulia 2006). The second concerns the ways in which religious beliefs, especially those about the gods' concerns with human conduct, encourage behaviors that are likely to make individuals trusted members of their social groups (e.g., Bering 2006). Whether their behaviors concern exhibitions of fidelity to the group and the group's gods, trustworthiness in moral matters, or both, the general proposal is that persons with such dispositions will, on average, have greater success obtaining resources and mates. Their compatriots will be more likely to enter into productive relationships—in all of the relevant senses—with such individuals, since their penchant for religious belief and deportment makes them good people with whom to cooperate. These circumstances should enable them to leave more copies of their genes, all else being equal, in the next generation.

Embracing explanatory pluralism inevitably produces pressures for broad interpretations of cognitive science, the fairly traditional conceptions of some theories in CSR notwithstanding (e.g., Lawson and McCauley 1990!). With regard to any particular explanatory question how narrowly or how widely cognition and the scientific enterprises that study it should be construed should turn primarily on the productivity of theoretical proposals, the empirical findings those proposals motivate, and how those theories and findings bear on the range of questions inquirers wish to explore. There is no such thing as a *complete explanation* in science. Thus, principled arguments for or against narrower or broader conceptions of cognitive science are probably misplaced. Instead of casting cognitive explanations exclusively in terms of internal rules and representations, 4E cognitive science stresses that cognition is typically embodied, enacted, embedded, and extended (Menary 2010). It surely is. For many purposes, including some that have arisen within CSR, however, 4E cognitive science is at least 1E too few.[10] The evidence that many forms of human cognition are *evolved* equals or exceeds that for any of the more celebrated E's (Buss 2005).

CSR theorists, who construe at least some religious belief and behavior as adaptations at the individual level, have enlisted methodological, theoretical, and evidential resources from evolutionary research in the biological sciences and, especially, in biological anthropology (e.g., Bulbulia and Sosis 2011). A particularly influential study for subsequent cognitive theorists has been a collaboration between Richard Sosis, a behavioral ecologist, and Bradley J. Ruffle, an economist, exploring the role of religious ritual in forging intragroup cooperation to the benefit, presumably, of each of the cooperators (Sosis and Ruffle 2003). The study exhibits how tools and methods from the social and cognitive sciences, viz., economic games, can be deployed to test such evolutionary hypotheses.

Sosis and Ruffle take advantage of existing arrangements in Israel to compare cooperation among members within religious as opposed to secular kibbutzim. They test the hypothesis that ritual participation builds cooperation. Current circumstances already lend indirect evidence to hypotheses about the beneficial effects of common religious affiliation. On virtually every relevant front (profitability, retention of members, longevity, etc.) religious kibbutzim on average fare better than do secular kibbutzim in contemporary Israel. Consequently, in order to have greater control on as many theoretically extraneous social and economic variables as possible, Sosis and Ruffle carried out the nonreligious half of their study in some of the most successful secular kibbutzim.

Sosis and Ruffle compared kibbutz members' performance in an economic game as a measure of their cooperativeness. They used real money in a common-pool resource dilemma game, in which two members of the same kibbutz play together anonymously. Both players know that the initial pool is 100 Israeli shekels (equivalent to about twenty-five US dollars) and that each of them will propose to withdraw some amount. The rules are simple. If the sum of the two players' proposed withdrawals exceeds 100 shekels, then neither player receives anything. If the sum of the two equals 100 shekels, then each player receives exactly the amount that he or she proposed to withdraw. If the sum of the two withdrawals is less than 100 shekels, then each player receives not only the amount that he or she proposed to withdraw but in addition three-fourths times whatever remains from the 100 shekels after both withdrawals have been made. Sosis and Ruffle presume that common-pool resource dilemma games are reasonably good models for the use of common resources, such as water or electricity, on a kibbutz. Crucially, both players stand to benefit more, if they can trust one another to make small withdrawals from the original 100 shekels.

Sosis and Ruffle's study revealed significant differences between the performances in this game of members from religious as opposed to secular kibbutzim. The members of religious kibbutzim withdrew significantly smaller amounts from the initial 100 shekel pool than did members of the secular kibbutzim. The study supplied further evidence, though, that this result may well have been the effect of participation in collective public rituals. In fact, the difference between the two groups was a function of the proposed withdrawals of the *male* members of the religious kibbutzim and, in particular, of the proposed withdrawals of the male members who participated in *collective public* ritual praying three times each day. Female players from religious kibbutzim did not propose withdrawals that differed significantly from those of players from secular kibbutzim. Although females in religious kibbutzim carry out rituals, those activities are mostly done domestically in private.

In some brief introductory comments, Sosis and Ruffle frame their findings in terms of costly signaling theory (e.g., Irons 2001). That theory proposes that participating in rituals communicates to other members an individual's commitment to the group. Basically, the more costly the ritual is, for example, costly initiation rites that include adopting group markers (Whitehouse 1996), the more convincing the signal is to the group. Participation in such rituals are hard-to-fake, high-cost signals to the community that the participants are reliable group members, who will not defect. After all, by participating in such rituals participants have paid a nontrivial cost in time, energy, and material resources. Both participating in the ritual and adopting group markers, such as scarification, characteristic clothing, or food taboos, requires that group members surrender various opportunities to pursue their own interests.

Since evolutionary thinking examines changes in large-scale systems over the long-term (McCauley 2009) rather than proximate cognitive mechanisms, much of that research is cognition-blind. The influence of Sosis and Ruffle's findings on subsequent research in CSR (e.g., Whitehouse and Lanman 2014), notwithstanding, in fact, they do not discuss cognition. Joseph Henrich (2009) stresses, however, that costly signaling theory leaves questions about proximate mechanisms unaddressed. Henrich notes that costly signaling theory does not tackle either the group dynamics or the historical processes from which such patterns arise. It also offers no account of the underlying psychological processes involved. It explains neither why costly requirements will increase commitments to beliefs, nor why costly signals seem less costly to insiders, nor when or why the production of costly signals reaches a ceiling.[11]

Henrich argues for the pivotal psychological role of credibility enhancing displays (CREDs) in explaining the import of costly signals. In addition to the *content* biases in cognition, which Boyer deploys so effectively to explain the character of religious representations, Henrich (2016) argues that human beings also possess evolved *context* biases in cognition as well. Specifically, *as cultural learners*, Henrich proposes that human beings have an evolved disposition to attend to prestigious individuals (Henrich and Gil-White 2001). Because prestigious people have either expertise in some area of human endeavor or sound judgment or both, prestigious people are good people to model. Focusing on CREDs, Henrich suggests, constitutes a kind of cultural immune system in that CREDs signal to cultural learners the models' reliability with regard to their avowed commitments to the group, to the cause, to the beliefs, and so on. Psychologically, the fact that everyone understands that cultural learners attend to models' CREDs (or lack thereof) decreases the possibilities that those models are self-interestedly manipulating cultural learners.

Certainly, costly signals are a variety of CREDs, but by no means do they exhaust the category. If prestigious models recommend some unfamiliar food and then, in fact, do such things as eat it themselves and feed it to their kin, they have not only exhibited a CRED, they and their kin have benefitted from the nourishment. Not all CREDs are costly. Preliminary experimentation with both adults and children indicates the value of CREDs for the cultural transmission of both practices and beliefs (Willard et al. n.d.).

CREDs explain the prominence and influence that leaders, who have made costly sacrifices, possess. Religious leaders, who forego wealth and sex or, in some cases, even their lives, demonstrate their good faith, so to speak, and increase the probabilities of the transmission of their religions. As Henrich comments (2016: 330), "CREDs can turn pain into pleasure and make martyrs into the most powerful of cultural transmitters." An evolved psychology of prestige underlies cultural learners' willingness to follow religious leaders who consistently produce CREDs.

Cognitive neuroscience

In their landmark article on cognitive science in the twentieth century, William Bechtel, Adele Abrahamsen, and George Graham (1998) stress that different disciplines among the several cognitive sciences enjoyed particular prominence for intervals across the time period in question. For example, the advent of the digital computer and the advances in computational theory after World War II endowed work in computer science and artificial intelligence during the first two decades of cognitive science with a certain pride of place. The prominence of the neurosciences in twenty-first-century cognitive science has also resulted from new technologies, though these have to do with brain imaging.

The ability to view structure and activity in human brains non-invasively has not only provided far more direct access to the central mechanisms of human cognition. It has also occasioned the development of inter-level theorizing and research integrating insights and findings from across the social, psychological, and brain sciences. These new imaging technologies have also furnished substantial, new bodies of evidence bearing on those hypotheses. Researchers from across the cognitive sciences have brought a variety of familiar tasks from experimental work in psychology and economics into the scanner to ascertain the impact of various stimuli on cognition and decision making. No work in CSR better illustrates such developments than Uffe Schjoedt and his colleagues' study (2011) of the influence of perceived charisma on the cognitive processing of believers (noted earlier in the third section).

Employing functional magnetic resonance imaging (fMRI), the Schjoedt team explored the effect of different speakers' perceived (religious) qualifications on listeners' responses to those speakers' spoken prayers. The researchers examined participants' responses to the spoken intercessory prayers of three individuals, whom they were told differed in their religious statuses. One was described as a non-Christian; the second was described as a Christian, and the third was described as a Christian "known for his healing powers" (Schjoedt et al. 2011: 120). (Assignments of these religious qualifications to the speakers were counter-balanced between participants.) Half of the participants were self-described Christian believers, while the other half were nonbelievers who were comparatively inexperienced with prayer and related religious matters. As a control the listeners also heard nonreligious speech with the same structure as prayer. Participants also responded to two questionnaires. The first, which was administered before the scan, assessed the character and level of their religiosity and experience with religious matters. The second, which was administered after the scan, inquired about their experiences of the three speakers in the experiment and of God's presence, while they were listening to the three.

Responses to the first questionnaire provided ample evidence for the religiosity of the religious participants, who held traditional beliefs with self-described conviction and who had considerable experience with standard religious forms and practices. By contrast, the secular participants did not believe in God, and they did not pray.

Responses to the second questionnaire indicated that the Christian participants rated the charisma of the reputed Christian speakers known for their healing powers significantly higher than that for the alleged non-Christian speakers, whereas the secular participants showed no significant differences between their ratings of the various speakers. The two groups showed even greater disparity with regard to their feelings of God's presence during the various prayers that they heard during the experiment.

To ascertain whether the researchers' hypothesis that participants' views of the various speakers' religious qualifications would have an impact on their neural activity, they compared activity levels across a host of the participants' brain areas, as measured by the blood oxygen level dependent (BOLD) imaging of their brains in fMRI scans. Their study uncovered a number of striking patterns.

Only the Christian participants' neural activity showed significant differences in their responses to the speakers and only in the contrast between the supposed non-Christian speakers and the speakers who were putatively

Christians known for having healing powers. To get a sense of the comparative size of the effects of these different speakers on the Christian participants' neural activity, Schjoedt and his colleagues compared activations in the five areas of participants' brains that showed the most extreme differences in response to the two speakers with their measures of baseline activity for those areas, which they had also obtained. Crucially, in all five areas, levels of neural activity were *less* than baseline for the Christian speakers known for their healing powers and *more* than baseline for the non-Christian speakers. These patterns also held for the Christian participants' responses to the post-scan questionnaires. Deactivation also correlated inversely with participants' reports about their feelings of God's presence, and the Christian participants' post-scan ratings of God's presence and of the speakers' charisma were strongly positively correlated.

The brain areas (medial prefrontal cortex, the temporoparietal junction, the temporopolar area, and the precuneus), which exhibited what the researchers described as "massive deactivation" in response to the reputed Christian speakers with healing abilities, concern social cognition and executive function. These are areas that are centrally involved in humans' negotiation of their complex social worlds and their experiences of decision making in that domain and others. The researchers note that their study involved a "passive paradigm," in which participants simply listened to the speakers praying without knowing that they would be asked to assess them afterward. The Schjoedt team (2011: 126) proposes that participants' "trust in passive paradigms down regulate executive and social cognitive processing, because [they] suspend or 'hand over' their critical faculty to the trusted person." Their Danish Christian participants rated the alleged Christian speakers with healing powers significantly more charismatic than the alleged non-Christian speakers. Schjoedt et al. (2011: 127) suggest that such down regulation of neural activity in these brain regions may well be an earmark of followers' susceptibility to charismatic authority.

Religious experience

Submission to charismatic authority may not leap to mind as a paradigmatic illustration of religious experience, but it is often a salient dimension of what happens to many people in the course of their religious lives. Theorists (e.g., Stark and Bainbridge 1996), besides Max Weber, accord considerable prominence to the influence of charismatic leaders in their general accounts of religion. Still, such features of people's religious experience seem pedestrian by comparison with the wondrous goings-on routinely reported by venerated religious figures, saints, and mystics.

The first theories in CSR, given their focus on the *transmission* of religious *ideas*, tended (at least compared to most other approaches in the study of religion) to downplay the importance of religious experience. The general contention (Sperber 1996) was that no matter how exhilarating or inspiring participants' experiences might prove, their transmission is always subject to *cognitive* constraints on religious representations' recognition, ability to attract attention, memorability, motivational impact, and communicability. Without packaging exhilaration and inspiration in a form that is readily transmittable, the relevant religious experiences are a good deal less likely to make any decisive differences in a religious system's fate.

Still, these theorists did not ignore religious experience altogether. Boyer (2001) noted that powerful emotions are frequently elicited automatically when engaging many of the domain specific cognitive capacities that religions target—from contamination avoidance to kin detection to fear of snakes and more. Even if their principal concerns were mnemonic matters, both Whitehouse (1996) and McCauley and Lawson (2002) were particularly interested in the emotional experiences that various religious rituals elicit in ritual patients. Again, though, such aspects of religious experience seem inconsequential when compared with the confrontations with the Cosmos, with the Holy, with the *Mysterium Tremendum* that many religious people supposedly go through.

For a variety of reasons, CSR has, more recently, turned its attentions to religious experience (e.g., Taves 2009). Beyond the traditional, widespread interest in the topic, ample evidence exists for package-able religious technologies (from rituals to disciplines to mind-altering drugs) that kindle some of those attention-grabbing experiences. Two considerations, however, are paramount. First, as the advocates of both 4E (and 6E!) cognitive science maintain, new tools and approaches (not just those of cognitive neuroscience) offer resources for understanding the experiential dimensions of our cognitive processing. Second, not only religious experience but its ability to intrigue are never going away. That the topic would resurface prominently in CSR was inevitable.

Dimitris Xygalatas, Ivana Konvalinka, and their colleagues' studies (Konvalinka et al. 2011; Xygalatas et al. 2011) of extreme rituals exemplify the sort of exciting new findings about the associated experiences that the tools of the cognitive sciences can produce. The Xygalatas-Konvalinka team studied a fire-walking ceremony that concludes the annual festival of San Juan in the small Spanish village of San Pedro Manrique. The fire-walking occurs at midnight on the summer solstice in an arena that was specially constructed for this ceremony and accommodates 3000 (approximately six times the population of the village). Earlier in the evening, the twenty-eight fire-walkers have processed through the village to the venue, accompanied by the townspeople. Over a half-hour, one by one the twenty-eight, usually carrying a friend or loved one on their backs, walked across a seven meter bed of hot coals, which reached temperatures of 677°C at the surface.

The Xygalatas-Konvalinka team recognized the exciting experimental opportunities in the natural (i.e., non-laboratory) setting that this fire-walking ceremony presents. After earning the trust of the village leadership, the local townspeople, and the fire-walkers themselves, they were permitted to introduce into the ceremony a number of controls and measurements that were unobtrusive and unproblematic from the standpoints of all involved. These included video recording equipment for the purpose of memory research (Xygalatas et al. 2013b), but, most important, for my purposes here, twelve fire-walkers as well as twenty-six spectators volunteered to wear heart-rate monitors. All of the volunteers wore the monitors during the roughly thirty minutes it took for the twenty-eight fire-walkers to traverse the coals as well as during a thirty minute interval one to three hours before the event (in order to obtain baseline heart-rate measures on all of the participants). Nine of the twenty-six spectators who wore the heart-rate monitors were either relatives or friends of one or more of the fire-walkers, while the other seventeen, recruited at random, were unknown to the fire-walkers.

Studying the correspondences between the fire-walkers and spectators' heart rates permitted the researchers to tease apart the synchronization of arousal in ritual from the synchronization of bodily movements. Considerable experimental evidence (e.g., Cohen et al. 2010) indicates that synchronized bodily movements create striking and similar responses among group members. Prolonged synchronous movements serve to align group members' cognitive states and levels of emotional arousal, which, in turn, are presumed to result in an elevated sense of group solidarity.

The empathetic projection hypothesis, at least in part, undergirds the second half of that story. That hypothesis holds that "it is the imagined responses of participants to focal events of the ritual that align their relevant cognitive states, without any strict need for orchestrated motor coordination" (Xygalatas et al. 2011: 735). The suggestion is that synchronization of bodily movement is not necessary for such outcomes but is only a particularly popular means for orchestrating arousal in common among group members. However it is achieved, it is the common *arousal* that is the underlying mechanism for the sort of empathetic responses that build pro-social feelings *among members of a group*.

The study offers more fine-grained scrutiny of the dynamics underlying that process. The Xygalatas-Konvalinka team suspected that, for people *affiliated* with one or more of the fire-walkers, simply observing a fire-walker might suffice to produce similar arousal. The findings they obtained from their study furnished stunning corroboration for that speculation. Crucially, the data they obtained from the heart-rate monitors "revealed striking *qualitative* similarities during the ritual between the heart rates of fire-walkers and heart rates of relatives and friends, with no apparent similarity to nonrelated spectators" (Konvalinka et al. 2011: 8515, emphasis added).

These findings are significant on at least two important fronts pertaining to the character of many people's religious experiences. First, they corroborated the empathetic projection hypothesis. Only the fire-walkers walked across the bed of hot coals, yet the heart rates of the spectators who identified themselves as either a relative or friend of a fire-walker did not differ significantly from the heart rates of the fire-walkers on all four of the heart-rate dynamics that the researchers measured. These affiliated spectators who participated in the study had no physical contact with the fire-walkers during their walks, but their heart rates tracked those of the fire-walkers not only during their walks but throughout the entire ceremony and, it turns out, even to some extent during the baseline epoch as well (Konvalinka et al. 2011: 8516–8517).

Second, the effect is, at least in part, a function of *social* relationships. It does *not* turn exclusively on the brain's mirroring capacities, which have attracted so much attention over the past two decades (Rizzolatti et al. 2011). Even though all of the spectators witnessed the fire-walking, it was only the heart rates of the spectators who were associates of a fire-walker that exhibited those qualitative similarities to the fire-walkers' heart rates. The non-affiliated spectators who participated in the study were no less capable of mirroring the fire-walkers' levels of arousal, as measured by their heart rates, but, in fact, they did not. Their heart rates on all four of the heart-rate dynamics that the researchers measured differed significantly from those of the fire-walkers.

The Xygalatas-Konvalinka team's study of the fire-walking at San Pedro Manrique provides a glimpse of the kinds of experimental controls, quantitative measures, descriptive precision, and *rich insights* that the theories and methods of CSR can supply for the study of at least some varieties of religious experience. On the one hand, their work contributes fundamentally to substantiating what are, in effect, theoretical proposals about religious experience from Religious Studies and the social sciences. On the other hand, this work and Xygalatas and his colleagues' subsequent work in Mauritius (e.g., Xygalatas et al. 2013a) also model for experimentalists in the social, psychological, and brain sciences how to carry on fruitful experimentation utilizing physiological measures in the field.

Afterword

Nothing seems more fitting and nothing delights me more than ending a book, which discusses some of the important philosophical issues occasioned by the pursuit of a cognitive science of religion, with this brief survey of some (but, by no means, all) of the most exciting experimental studies that now animate the field and lead it into new areas of endeavor. In light of such work, neither CSR's success nor its promise—as an ever-growing body of methods, theories, and findings for illuminating what we regard as religious phenomena and for enriching their study—is any longer a matter of debate. *Sometimes*, and the case of the cognitive science of religion is one of those times, it is a good thing that science does not get waylaid by Religious Studies scholars' philosophical worries.

Notes

Chapter 2

1   This is not to say that they are completely different. (To repeat—all distinctions, except for those of logic, fall on some semantic continuum.)

Chapter 3

1   Greater sensitivity on the part of some historians of religion to the place of the study of religion among the cognitive and social sciences is increasingly evident. For example, at a recent conference in Poland a number of scholars in the history of religions released a statement endorsing a shift of attention to the cognitive and social sciences. An explicit agenda of this paper is to encourage this new trend (Wiebe 1984, 1985, 1988; Proudfoot 1985; Penner 1989; Segal 1989).

2   If these were bureaucratic arguments (where is the discipline housed, who funds it, etc.), then we would be sympathetic with autonomy claims because anyone with something interesting and important to do needs space and support. The claims, however, are obviously not merely bureaucratic but methodological as well because they involve conceptual issues about the best way to study the subject matter, the nature of the theoretical object, the relationships among different approaches, and so on.

3   There is also a deep tension in these two quotes from Otto. In the first (in near imitation of Kant's project), he implies that we are dealing with what seems, virtually, to be a faculty of *a priori* status. In the second quote, he concedes that for some this (apparent) faculty has had no impact whatsoever on the character of human experience (in striking contrast to the apparent allusion to Kantian modes of thought and expression).

4   We are indebted to Michael Pye and Donald Wiebe for this metaphor.

5   We are more positive about the social sciences than Hans Penner, who sometimes seems to come close to equating functionalism and social science:

"Functionalism can be viewed as the theory for explaining things in *the* social sciences" (Penner 1989: 106) and less positive than Donald Wiebe (1984, 1985, 1988). For a defense of functionalism, see McCauley and Lawson (1984).

Chapter 4

1   In this paper, we will follow the American philosopher's convention of referring to concepts by enclosing the corresponding terms for the concepts in single quotes. Thus, 'culture' refers to the concept of culture.

2   We are pragmatists about ontology. Claims for the autonomy of culture fare neither better nor worse than the relative *explanatory* success of theories that confine themselves to quintessentially cultural concepts and those—addressing the same phenomena—that do not. To the extent such theories address the intellectual and practical problems that provoked such inquiries in the first place, their ontological posits merit our allegiance.

3   It follows, incidentally, that the postmodernist trappings surrounding this movement are largely incidental. All of the pivotal philosophical commitments were already present in anthropology's hermeneutic turn twenty-five years ago.

4   We should clarify from the outset that we enthusiastically endorse being more informed rather than less about anything anyone seeks to study.

5   Consider, for example, the claim that emotions are not merely culturally constrained but are culturally *constituted*: "The point then is not how *much* culture matters. For culture does not constitute emotions by degree. The point is *how* culture matters. For culture is the assemblage of those discourses *within which the emotions come to be*" (McCarthy 1994: 277, some emphasis added).

6   Whatever *that* is. Recall Gellner's claim that meaning is the *problem* not the solution in the study of culture.

7   See Humphrey and Laidlaw (1994) for but the most recent expression of this view.

8   The problem, though, is that no one has provided an even remotely convincing theory that offers a unified account of these phenomena. Humphrey and Laidlaw (1994) advance an account of the ritualization of action that is frequently suggestive. They concede fairly openly, though, that their approach makes good sense of "liturgy-centered" rituals only, forcing them to treat "performance-centered" rituals as peripheral cases at best. (This already disqualifies their discussion as an example of a theory of ritual-in-general—a disqualification which they straightforwardly acknowledge.)

Even as an account of liturgical rituals, Humphrey and Laidlaw's position faces some nagging problems. The most important, to our minds, concerns their insistence that nothing constrains the ordering of ritual segments in liturgical rituals. As evidence they note that the ordering of ritual segments in the Jain *puja* has undergone virtually unlimited variation over time.

But this is not even a sufficient defense of the claim's plausibility, let alone its truth. First, evidence concerning but one set of rituals from one cultural system hardly counts as compelling in the face of what seem to be hundreds of counter-instances from other cultures. Second, even in the case of the *puja*, from the fact that it displays variations in the ordering of ritual segments over time, it does not follow that in any given performance the order is not constrained. No doubt, over time, word order has undergone variation in (probably) all natural languages. It does not follow that at any given time word order is not heavily constrained.

Chapter 5

1   Its currency notwithstanding, grammaticality is almost certainly too strong
     a standard to employ here for two reasons. First, from a practical standpoint,
     the critical question usually is whether or not an audience comprehends the
     speaker's utterance well enough to respond in the fashion the speaker desires.
     This criterion for the acceptability of an utterance often falls a good deal short
     of what we typically regard as grammatical usage. Second, from a theoretical
     standpoint, "grammaticality" carries connotations that are chiefly syntactic.
     Often, though, speakers' normative judgments about the acceptability of
     linguistic strings do not turn exclusively on syntactic considerations.

Chapter 6

1   Oddly, many interpretivists do not object when psychoanalytically oriented
     thinkers make similar claims on the basis of far *less* evidence arising from
     carefully designed tests.
2   However pointed the criticisms, the controversies (Norenzayan 2014; Staussberg
     2014) that have swirled around the synthetic proposals of Ara Norenzayan's *Big
     Gods* (2013) illustrate the sort of constructive exchanges that the interaction of

CSR and Religious Studies can yield. None of the issues are settled. All of the auditors and, I suspect, all of the participants as well have benefitted.

3   That, however, is not to imply that the scientific community is unconcerned with the moral and political implications of its work. Organizations such as the Union of Concerned Scientists and the Center for Science in the Public Interest have played a valuable and constructive role in enhancing public understanding of scientific issues and in contributing to thoughtful public policies.

4   Postmodernists' worries about the status of texts were not a mere coincidence.

5   During that time, CSR has arisen as a recognized contributor in Religious Studies with formal representation in some of the world's largest professional societies (International Association for the History of Religions, American Academy of Religion), a professional society of its own (International Association for the Cognitive Science of Religion—IACSR), and specialized journals (*Journal of the Cognitive Science of Religion, Journal of Cognition and Culture, Religion, Brain & Behavior, Journal of Cognitive Historiography*). At the same time, it has also become a notable subfield within cognitive science with the IACSR regularly meeting periodically with and receiving formal recognition and support from the Cognitive Science Society, with papers and posters in the field accepted at that society's annual meetings and with relevant articles by eminent mainstream cognitive scientists appearing in its flagship journal, *Cognitive Science* (Astuti and Harris 2008; Banerjee et al. 2013; Legare and Souza 2014).

6   Exactly how direct the roles of such theory of mind capacities and of promiscuous teleology are in any such intuitive theism is a point of controversy (Lindeman et al. 2015).

7   This includes the radically counter-intuitive representations in which the sciences traffic (McCauley 2011).

8   For an extended, systematic treatment of the issues at stake, see Barrett (2008).

9   Referring to these as "maximally counter-intuitive" representations is an unhelpful convention (e.g., Norenzayan et al. 2006). Obviously, the number of violations exceeds one, but this hardly makes them *maximally* counter-intuitive.

10 Arguably, it is probably 2E's too few. In addition to the importance of attending to cognition as *evolved*, it seems worthwhile to recognize how richly textured cognition is *emotionally* as well (Thagard 2006).

11 Henrich's observations illustrate lessons of explanatory pluralism: science does not traffic in comprehensive explanations; the vindication of an explanatory theory simply occasions a new set of questions about its un-explicated details and its further implications.

References

Astuti, R. and Harris, P. L. (2008), "Understanding Mortality and the Life of the Ancestors in Rural Madagascar," *Cognitive Science*, 32: 713–740.

Atkinson, Q. D. and Whitehouse, H. (2010), "The Cultural Morphospace of Ritual Form: Examining Modes of Religiosity Cross-Culturally," *Evolution and Human Behavior*, 32(1): 50–62.

Atran, S. and Henrich, J. (2010), "The Evolution of Religion: How Cognitive By-products, Adaptive Learning Heuristics, Ritual Displays, and Group Competition Generate Deep Commitments to Prosocial Religions," *Biological Theory*, 5: 18–30.

Banerjee, K., Haque, O., and Spelke, E. (2013), "Melting Lizards and Crying Mailboxes: Children's Preferential Recall of Minimally Counterintuitive Concepts," *Cognitive Science*, 37(7): 1251–1289.

Baranowski, A. (1994), *Ritual Alone: Cognition and Meaning of Patterns of Time* (Doctoral Dissertation). Available at: http://onesearch.library.utoronto.ca/

Barkow, J. H., Cosmides, L., and Tooby, J. (eds) (1992), *The Adapted Mind: Evolutionary Psychology and the Generation of Culture*, New York: Oxford University Press.

Barrett, H. C. (2015), *The Shape of Thought: How Mental Adaptations Evolve*, New York: Oxford University Press.

Barrett, J. L. (1998), "Cognitive Constraints on Hindu Concepts of the Divine," *Journal for the Scientific Study of Religion*, 37: 608–619.

Barrett, J. L. (2008), "Coding and Quantifying Counterintuitiveness in Religious Concepts: Theoretical and Methodological Reflections," *Method and Theory in the Study of Religion*, 20: 308–338.

Barrett, J. L. (2012), *Born Believers: The Science of Children's Religious Belief*, New York: Free Press.

Barrett, J. and Keil, F. (1996), "Conceptualizing a Non-natural Entity: Anthropomorphism in God Concepts," *Cognitive Psychology*, 31: 219–247.

Barrett, J. L. and Lawson, E. T. (2001), "Ritual Intuitions: Cognitive Contributions to Judgments of Ritual Efficacy," *Journal of Cognition and Culture*, 1: 183–201.

Barrett, J. L. and Nyhof, M. A. (2001), "Spreading Non-natural Concepts: The Role of Intuitive Conceptual Structures in Memory and Transmission of Cultural Materials," *Journal of Cognition and Culture*, 1(1): 69–100.

Barrett, J. L., Richert, R. A., and Driesenga, A. (2001), "God's Beliefs versus Mother's: The Development of Non-human Agent Concepts," *Child Development*, 72: 50–65.

Barth, F. (1987), *Cosmologies in the Making: A Generative Approach to Cultural Variation in Inner New Guinea*, Cambridge: Cambridge University Press.

Bechtel, W. (ed.) (1986), *Integrating Scientific Disciplines*, The Hague: Martinus Nijhoff.

Bechtel, W. (2006), *Discovering Cell Mechanisms: The Creation of Modern Cell Biology*, New York: Cambridge University Press.

Bechtel, W. (2007), "Reducing Psychology While Maintaining Its Autonomy via Mechanistic Explanation," in M. Shouten and H. Looren de Jong (eds), *The Matter of the Mind: Philosophical Essays on Psychology, Neuroscience, and Reduction*, 172–198, Oxford: Blackwell Publishers.

Bechtel, W. and Richardson, R. C. (1993), *Discovering Complexity: Decomposition and Localization as Strategies in Scientific Research*, Princeton, NJ: Princeton University Press.

Bechtel, W., Abrahamsen, A. A., and Graham, G. (1998), "The Life of Cognitive Science," in W. Bechtel and G. Graham (eds), *Blackwell Companion to Cognitive Science*, 1–104, Oxford: Blackwell Publishers.

Bell, C. (2005), "Theory, Palm Trees, and Mere Being," *Criterion*, 44: 2–11.

Bering, J. M. (2006), "The Folk Psychology of Souls," *Behavioral and Brain Sciences*, 29: 453–498.

Bering, J. M. and Bjorklund, D. F. (2004), "The Natural Emergence of Reasoning about the Afterlife as a Developmental Regularity," *Developmental Psychology*, 40(2): 217–233.

Bering, J., Blasi, C. H., and Bjorklund, D. F. (2005), "The Development of 'Afterlife' Beliefs in Religiously and Secularly Schooled Children," *British Journal of Developmental Psychology*, 23: 587–607.

Bickle, J. (1998), *Psychoneural Reduction: The New Wave*, Cambridge: The MIT Press.

Bickle, J. (2003), *Philosophy and Neuroscience: A Ruthlessly Reductive Account*, Dordrecht: Kluwer Academic Publishers.

Bleeker, C. (1975), *The Rainbow: A Collection of Studies in the Science of Religion*, Leiden: Brill.

Bloor, D. (1981), "The Strengths of the Strong Programme," *Philosophy of Social Science*, 2: 199–213.

Boas, F. (1963), *The Mind of Primitive Man*, New York: Collier Books.

Boyd, R. and Richerson, P. J. (1985), *Culture and the Evolutionary Process*, Chicago, IL: University of Chicago Press.

Boyer, P. (1990), *Tradition as Truth and Communication*, Cambridge: Cambridge University Press.

Boyer, P. (1993), *Cognitive Aspects of Religious Symbolism*, Cambridge: Cambridge University Press.

Boyer, P. (1994), *The Naturalness of Religious Ideas*, Berkeley: University of California Press.

Boyer, P. (2001), *Religion Explained: The Evolutionary Origins of Religious Thought*, New York: Basic Books.

Boyer, P. and Liénard, P. (2006), "Precaution Systems and Ritualized Behavior," *Behavioral and Brain Sciences*, 29(6): 595–650.

Boyer, P. and Ramble, C. (2001), "Cognitive Templates for Religious Concepts: Cross-Cultural Evidence for Recall of Counter-Intuitive Representations," *Cognitive Science*, 25(4): 535–564.

Boyer, P. and Walker, S. (2000), "Intuitive Ontology and Cultural Input in the Acquisition of Religious Concepts," in K. S. Rosengren, C. N. Johnson, and P. L. Harris (eds), *Imagining the Impossible: The Development of Magical, Scientific, and Religious Thinking in Contemporary Society*, 130–156, Cambridge: Cambridge University Press.

Brewer, W. (1974), "There Is No Convincing Evidence for Operant or Classical Conditioning in Adult Humans," in W. B. Weimer and D. S. Palermo (eds), *Cognition and Symbolic Processes*, 1–42, New York: John Wiley and Sons.

Bromberger, S. (1966), "Why Questions," in R. Colodny (eds), *Mind and Cosmos: Explorations in the Philosophy of Science*, 86–111, Pittsburgh, PA: University of Pittsburgh Press.

Brown, H. (1979), *Perception, Theory and Commitment*, Chicago, IL: University of Chicago Press.

Bruner, E. M. (1994), "Abraham Lincoln as Authentic Reproduction: A Critique of Postmodernism," *American Anthropologist*, 96: 397–415.

Buckley, J. and Buckley, T. (1995), "Response: Anthropology, History of Religions, and a Cognitive Approach to Religious Phenomena," *Journal of the American Academy of Religion*, 63: 343–352.

Bulbulia, J. (2004), "The Cognitive and Evolutionary Psychology of Religion," *Biology and Philosophy*, 18(5): 655–686.

Bulbulia, J. (2006), "Nature's Medicine: Religiosity as an Adaptation for Health and Cooperation," in P. MacNamara (ed.), *Where Man and God Meet: The New Sciences of Religion and Brain*, 87–121, Westwood, CT: Greenwood Publishers.

Bulbulia, J. and Sosis, R. (2011), "Signalling Theory and the Evolution of Religious Cooperation," *Religion*, 41(3): 363–388.

Burkert, W. (1996), *Creation of the Sacred: Tracks of Biology in Early Religions*, Cambridge: Harvard University Press.

Buss, D. M. (ed.) (2005), *The Handbook of Evolutionary Psychology*, New York: Wiley.

Carnap, R. (1936–1937), "Testability and Meaning," *Philosophy of Science*, 3: 1–40.

Casler, K. and Kelemen, D. (2008), "Developmental Continuity in Teleo-functional Explanation: Reasoning about Nature among Romanian Romani Adults," *Journal of Cognition and Development*, 9(3): 340–362.

Causey, R. (1977), *Unity of Science*, Dordrecht: Reidel.

Chomsky, N. (1959), "Review of Verbal Behavior," *Language*, 35: 26–58.

Chomsky, N. (1972), *Language and Mind*, New York: Harcourt, Brace, and Jovanovich.

Churchland, P. M. (1979), *Scientific Realism and the Plasticity of Mind*, Cambridge: Cambridge University Press.

Churchland, P. M. (1981). "Eliminative Materialism and the Propositional Attitudes," *Journal of Philosophy*, 78(2): 67–90.

Churchland, P. M. (1988), *Matter and Consciousness: A Contemporary Introduction to the Philosophy of Mind* (Rev. ed.), Cambridge: The MIT Press.

Churchland, P. M. (1989), *A Neurocomputational Perspective: The Nature of Mind and the Structure of Science*, Cambridge: The MIT Press.

Churchland, P. S. (1983), "Consciousness: The Transmutation of a Concept," *Pacific Philosophical Quarterly*, 64: 80–93.

Churchland, P. S. (1986), *Neurophilosophy*, Cambridge: The MIT Press.

Churchland, P. S. (1988), "Reduction and the Neurological Basis of Consciousness," in A. J. Marcel and E. Bisiach (eds), *Consciousness in Contemporary Science*, 273–304, Oxford: Oxford University Press.

Churchland, P. M. and Churchland, P. S. (1990), "Intertheoretic Reduction: A Neuroscientist's Field Guide," *Seminars in the Neurosciences*, 2: 249–256.

Churchland, P. M. and Churchland, P. S. (1996), "Replies from the Churchlands," in R. N. McCauley (ed.), *The Churchlands and Their Critics*, 217–311, Oxford: Blackwell Publishers.

Clifford, J. and Marcus, G. (1986), *Writing Culture: The Poetics and Politics of Ethnography*, Berkeley: University of California Press.

Cohen, E. (2007), *The Mind Possessed: The Cognition of Spirit Possession in an Afro-Brazilian Religious Tradition*, Oxford: Oxford University Press.

Cohen, E. and Barrett, J. L. (2008a), "Conceptualizing Spirit Possession: Ethnographic and Experimental Evidence," *Ethos*, 36: 246–267. DOI: 10.1111/j.1548 -1352.2008.00013.x.

Cohen, E. and Barrett, J. L. (2008b), "When Minds Migrate: Conceptualizing Spirit Possession," *Journal of Cognition and Culture*, 8: 23–48.

Cohen, E., Ejsmond-Frey, R., Knight, N., and Dunbar, R. I. M. (2010), "Rowers' High: Behavioural Synchrony Is Correlated with Elevated Pain Thresholds," *Biology Letters*, 6(1): 106–108.

Cole, M. and Scribner, S. (1974), *Culture and Thought: A Psychological Introduction*, New York: Wiley.

Cosmides, L. (1989), "The Logic of Social Exchange: Has Natural Selection Shaped How Humans Reason? Studies with the Wason Selection Task," *Cognition*, 31(3): 187–276.

Craver, C. F. (2007), *Explaining the Brain*, Oxford: Oxford University Press.

Craver, C. F. and Bechtel, W. (2007), "Top-down Causation without Top-down Causes," *Biology and Philosophy*, 22: 547–563.

Cummins, R. (1983), *The Nature of Psychological Explanation*, Cambridge: The MIT Press.

Cummins, R. (2000), "How Does It Work? versus What Are the Laws?: Two Conceptions of Psychological Explanation," in F. Keil and R. Wilson (eds), *Explanation and Cognition*, 117–144, Cambridge: The MIT Press.

Czachesz, I. and Uro, R. (eds) (2013), *Mind, Morality and Magic: Cognitive Science Approaches in Biblical Studies*, Durham: Acumen.

Dale, R., Dietrich, E., and Chemero, A. (2009), "Explanatory Pluralism in Cognitive Science," *Cognitive Science*, 33: 739–742.

Dehaene, S., and Mehler, J. (1992), "Cross-linguistic Regularities in the Frequency of Number Words," *Cognition*, 43: 1–29.

Doniger, W. (1988), *Other Peoples' Myths: The Cave of Echoes*, New York: Macmillan.

Durkheim, E. (1964), *The Rules of Sociological Method*, translated by J. Mueller and S. Soloway, New York: The Free Press of Glenco.

Durkheim, E. (1965), *The Elementary Forms of the Religious Life*, New York: Free Press.

Eliade, M. (1961), *The Sacred and the Profane*, New York: Harper and Row.

Eliade, M. (1963), *Patterns of Comparative Religion*, Cleveland, OH: World Publishing Company.

Endicott, R. P. (1998), "Collapse of the New Wave," *Journal of Philosophy*, 95: 53–72.

Evans, E. M. (2000), "Beyond Scopes: Why Creationism Is Here to Stay," in F. Keil and R. Wilson (eds), *Imagining the Impossible: The Development of Magical, Scientific, and Religious Thinking in Contemporary Society*, 305–333, Cambridge: Cambridge University Press.

Evans, E. M. (2001), "Cognitive and Contextual Factors in the Emergence of Diverse Belief Systems: Creationism versus Evolution," *Cognitive Psychology*, 42: 217–266.

Feyerabend, P. K. (1962), "Explanation, Reduction, and Empiricism," in H. Feigl and G. Maxwell (eds), *Minnesota Studies in the Philosophy of Science: Vol. 3*, 28–97, Minneapolis: University of Minnesota Press.

Feyerabend, P. K. (1975), *Against Method*, London: NLB.

Fitzgerald, T. (2000), *The Ideology of Religious Studies*, New York: Oxford University Press.

Fodor, J. A. (1983), *The Modularity of Mind*, Cambridge: The MIT Press.

Freud, S. (1927/1961), *The Future of an Illusion*, translated by W. D. Robson-Scott, New York: Anchor.

Gazzaniga, M. (ed.) (1988), *Perspectives in Memory Research*, Cambridge: The MIT Press.

Geertz, C. (1973), *The Interpretation of Cultures*, New York: Basic Books.

Geertz, C. (1988), *Works and Lives*, Stanford: Stanford University Press.

Gellner, E. (1988), "The Stakes in Anthropology," *American Scholar*, 57: 17–30.

Ginges, J., Hansen, I., and Norenzayan, A. (2009), "Religion and Support of Suicide Attacks," *Psychological Science*, 20: 224–230.

Gonce, L. O., Upal, M. A., Slone, D. J., and Tweney, R. D. (2006), "Role of Context in the Recall of Counterintuitive Concepts," *Journal of Cognition and Culture*, 6(3–4): 521–547.

Goody, J. (1961), "Religion and Ritual: The Definition Problem," *British Journal of Psychology*, 12: 143–164.

Gould, S. J. (1981), *The Mismeasure of Man*, New York: Norton.

Graham, J., Haidt, J., Koleva, S., Motyl, M., Iyer, R., Wojcik, S., and Ditto, P. H. (2013), "Moral Foundations Theory: The Pragmatic Validity of Moral Pluralism," *Advances in Experimental Social Psychology*, 47: 55–130.

Grunbaum, A. (1984), *The Foundations of Psychoanalysis: A Philosophical Critique*, Berkeley: University of California Press.

Guthrie, S. (1980), "A Cognitive Theory of Religion," *Current Anthropology*, 21(2): 181–203.

Guthrie, S. (1993), *Faces in the Clouds*, Oxford: Oxford University Press.

Harmon-Vukić, M. E. and Slone, D. J. (2009), "The Effect of Integration on the Recall of Counterintuitive Stories," *Journal of Cognition and Culture*, 9: 57–68.

Harmon-Vukić, M. E., Upal, M. A., and Sheehan, K. J. (2012), "Understanding the Memory Advantage of Counterintuitive Concepts," *Religion, Brain & Behavior*, 2(2): 121–139.

Harris, P. L. and Gimenéz, M. (2005), "Children's Acceptance of Conflicting Testimony: The Case of Death," *Journal of Cognition and Culture*, 5: 143–164.

Hempel, C. (1965), *Aspects of Scientific Explanation*, New York: The Free Press.

Henrich, J. (2009), "The Evolution of Costly Displays, Cooperation and Religion: Credibility Enhancing Displays and Their Implications for Cultural Evolution," *Evolution and Human Behavior*, 30(4): 244–260.

Henrich, J. (2016), *The Secret of Our Success: How Culture Is Driving Our Evolution, Domesticating Our Species, and Making Us Smarter*, Princeton, NJ: Princeton University Press.

Henrich, J. and Gil-White, F. J. (2001), "The Evolution of Prestige: Freely Conferred Status as a Mechanism for Enhancing the Benefits of Cultural Transmission," *Evolution and Human Behavior*, 22(3): 1–32.

Hirst, W. and Gazzaniga, M. S. (1988), "Present and Future of Memory Research and Its Applications," in M. S. Gazzaniga (ed.), *Perspectives in Memory Research*, 279–308, Cambridge: The MIT Press.

Hodge, K. M. (2011), "On Imagining the Afterlife," *Journal of Cognition and Culture*, 11(3–4): 367–389.

Hooker, C. (1981), "Towards a General Theory of Reduction," *Dialogue*, 20: 38–59, 201–236, 496–529.

Horton, R. (1967), "African Traditional Thought and Western Science," *Africa: Journal of the International African Institute*, 37: 50–71.

Humphrey, C. L. and Laidlaw, J. (1994), *The Archetypal Actions of Ritual*, Oxford: Oxford University Press.

Irons W. (2001), "Religion as a Hard-to-fake Sign of Commitment," in Nesse R. (ed.), *Evolution and the Capacity for Commitment*, 292–309, New York: Russell Sage Foundation.

James, W. (1902/1929), *The Varieties of Religious Experience*, New York: The Modern Library.

Jarvie, I. (1972), *Concepts and Society*, London: Routledge and Kegan Paul.

Kaplan, D. and Manners, R. (1972), *Culture Theory*, Englewood Cliffs: Prentice-Hall.

Keesing, R. M. (1987), "Anthropology as Interpretive Quest," *Current Anthropology*, 28: 161–169.

Keil, F. C. (1979), *Semantic and Conceptual Development*, Cambridge: Harvard University Press.

Keil, F. C. (1989), *Concepts, Kinds, and Conceptual Development*, Cambridge: The MIT Press.

Kelemen, D. (1999a), "The Scope of Teleological Thinking in Pre-School Children," *Cognition*, 70(3): 241–272.

Kelemen, D. (1999b), "Why Are Rocks Pointy?: Children's Preference for Teleological Explanations of the Natural World," *Developmental Psychology*, 35(6): 1440–1452.

Kelemen, D. (2004), "Are Children 'Intuitive Theists'?: Reasoning about Purpose and Design in Nature," *Psychological Science*, 15: 295–301.

Kelemen, D. and Rosset, Evelyn. (2009), "The Human Function Compunction: Teleological Explanation in Adults," *Cognition*, 111(1): 138–143.

Kelemen, D., Rottman, J., and Seston, R. (2013), "Professional Physical Scientists Display Tenacious Teleological Tendencies: Purpose-based Reasoning as a Cognitive Default," *Journal of Experimental Psychology: General*, 142(4): 1074–1083.

Konvalinka, I., Xygalatas, D., Bulbulia, J., Schjoedt, U., Jegindø, E.-M., Wallot, S., Van Orden, G., and Roepstorff, A. (2011), "Synchronized Arousal Between Performers and Related Spectators in a Fire-walking Ritual," *Proceedings of the National Academy of Sciences*, 108(20): 8514–8519.

Kuhn, T. (1970), *The Structure of Scientific Revolutions* (2nd ed.), Chicago, IL: University of Chicago Press.

Lakoff, G. (1987), *Women, Fire, and Dangerous Things*, Chicago, IL: University of Chicago Press.

Lakoff, G. and Johnson, M. L. (1980), *Metaphors We Live By*, Chicago, IL: University of Chicago Press.

Langacker, R. (1987), *Foundations of Cognitive Grammar*, Stanford, CA: Stanford University Press.

Laudan, L. (1977), *Progress and Its Problems*, Berkeley: University of California Press.

Lawson, E. T. and McCauley, R. N. (1990), *Rethinking Religion: Connecting Cognition and Culture*, Cambridge: Cambridge University Press.

Lawson, E. T. and McCauley, R. N. (1993), "Crisis of Conscience, Riddle of Identity: Making Space for a Cognitive Approach to Religious Phenomena," *Journal of the American Academy of Religion*, 61: 201–223.

Lawson, E. T. and McCauley, R. N. (1995), "Caring for the Details: A Humane Reply to Buckley and Buckley," *Journal of the American Academy of Religion*, 63: 353–357.

Lawson, E. T. and Wiebe, D. (1989), "The Study of Religion in Its Social-scientific Context: A Perspective on the 1989 Warsaw Conference on Methodology," *Method and Theory in the Study of Religion*, 12(1): 98–101.

Legare, C. H. and Souza, A. (2014), "Searching for Control: Priming Randomness Increases the Evaluation of Ritual Efficacy," *Cognitive Science*, 38: 152–161.

Lesche, C. (1985), "Is Psychoanalysis Therapeutic Technique or Scientific Research? A Metascientific Investigation," in K. B. Madsen and L. P. Mos (eds), *Annals of Theoretical Psychology: Vol. 3*, 157–217, New York: Plenum Press.

Liénard, P. and Boyer, P. (2006), "Why Cultural Rituals? A Cultural Selection Model of Ritualized Behaviour," *American Anthropologist*, 108(4): 814–827.

Lindeman, M., Svedholm-Häkkinen, A. M., and Lipsanen, J. (2015), "Ontological Confusions but Not Mentalizing Abilities Predict Religious Belief, Paranormal Belief, and Belief in Supernatural Purpose," *Cognition*, 134: 63–76.

Long, C. (1986), *Significations*, Minneapolis, MN: Fortress.

Looren de Jong, H. and Schouten, M. (2007), "Mind Reading and Mirror Neurons: Exploring Reduction," in M. Schouten and H. Looren de Jong (eds), *The Matter of the Mind: Philosophical Essays on Psychology, Neuroscience and Reduction*, 298–322, Oxford: Blackwell Publishers.

Lumsden, C. J. and Wilson, E. O. (1981), *Genes, Minds, and Culture*, Cambridge: Harvard University Press.

Madigan, S. A. (1969), "Intraserial Repetition and Coding Processes in Free Recall," *Journal of Verbal Learning and Verbal Behavior*, 8(6): 828–835.

Makkreel, R. (1985), "Dilthey and Universal Hermeneutics: The Status of the Human Sciences," *Journal of the British Society for Phenomenology*, 16: 236–249.

Martin, L. H. (2015), *The Mind of Mithraists: Historical and Cognitive Studies in the Roman Cult of Mithras*, London: Bloomsbury.

Martin, L. H. and Sørensen, J. (eds) (2011), *Past Minds: Studies in Cognitive Historiography*, London: Equinox.

Martin, L. H. and Wiebe, D. (2012), "Religious Studies as a Scientific Discipline: The Persistence of a Delusion," *Journal of the American Academy of Religion*, 80(3): 587–597.

McCarthy, E. D. (1994). "The Social Construction of Emotions: New Directions from Culture Theory," *Social Perspectives on Emotion*, 2: 267-279.

McCauley, R. N. (1986a), "Intertheoretic Relations and the Future of Psychology," *Philosophy of Science*, 53: 179–199.

McCauley, R. N. (1986b), "Searching for a Fully Scientific Psychology," *Contemporary Psychology*, 31: 844–845.

McCauley, R. N. (1992), "Models of Knowing and Their Relations to Our Understanding of Liberal Education," *Metaphilosophy*, 23: 288–309.

McCauley, R. N. (1996), "Explanatory Pluralism and the Coevolution of Theories in Science," in R. N. McCauley (ed.), *The Churchlands and Their Critics*, 17–47, Oxford: Blackwell Publishers.

McCauley, R. N. (2000), "Overcoming Barriers to a Cognitive Psychology of Religion," *Method and Theory in the Study of Religion*, 12: 141–161, in special issue A. Geertz and R. McCutcheon (eds), *Perspectives on Method and Theory in the Study of Religion*, The Hague: Brill.

McCauley, R. N. (2007), "Reduction: Models of Cross-Scientific Relations and Their Implications for the Psychology-Neuroscience Interface," in P. Thagard (ed.), *Handbook of the Philosophy of Psychology and Cognitive Science*, 105–158, Amsterdam: Elsevier.

McCauley, R. N. (2009), "Time Is of the Essence: Explanatory Pluralism and Accommodating Theories About Long Term Processes," *Philosophical Psychology*, 22: 611–635.

McCauley, R. N. (2011), *Why Religion Is Natural and Science Is Not*, New York: Oxford University Press.

McCauley, R. N. (2012), "The Importance of Being 'Ernest'," in E. Slingerland and M. Collard (eds), *Integrating the Sciences and Humanities: Interdisciplinary Approaches*, 266–281, New York: Oxford University Press.

McCauley, R. N. (2013), "Explanatory Pluralism and the Cognitive Science of Religion: Or Why Scholars in Religious Studies Should Stop Worrying about Reductionism," in D. Xygalatas and W. W. McCorkle, Jr (eds), *Mental Culture: Classical Social Theory and the Cognitive Science of Religion*, 11–32, London: Acumen.

McCauley, R. N. (n.d.), Cross-scientific Relations and the Study of the Emotions.

McCauley, R. N. and Bechtel, W. (2001), "Explanatory Pluralism and the Heuristic Identity Theory," *Theory and Psychology*, 11: 738–761.

McCauley, R. N. and Lawson, E. T. (1984), "Functionalism Reconsidered," *History of Religions*, 23: 372–381.

McCauley, R. N. and Lawson, E. T. (1993), "Connecting the Cognitive and the Cultural: Artificial Minds as Methodological Devices in the Study of the Sociocultural," in R. Burton (ed.), *Minds: Natural and Artificial*, 121–145, Albany: State University of New York Press.

McCauley, R. N. and Lawson, E. T. (1996), "Who Owns 'Culture'?" *Method and Theory in the Study of Religion*, 8(2): 171–190.

McCauley, R. N. and Lawson, E. T. (1998), "Interactionism and the Non-Obviousness of Scientific Theories," *Method and Theory in the Study of Religion*, 10: 61–77.

McCauley, R. N. and Lawson, E. T. (2002), *Bringing Ritual to Mind: Psychological Foundations of Cultural Forms*, Cambridge: Cambridge University Press.

McMullin, E. (1978), "Structural Explanation," *American Philosophical Quarterly*, 15: 139–147.

Menary, R. A. (2010), "Introduction to the Special Issue on 4E Cognition," *Phenomenology and the Cognitive Sciences*, 9(4): 459–463.

Mishkin, M., Ungerleider, L. G., and Macko, K. A. (1983), "Object Vision and Spatial Vision: Two Cortical Pathways," *Trends in Neurosciences*, 6: 414–417.

Mitchell, M. (2009), *Complexity: A Guided Tour*, New York: Oxford University Press.

Morinis, A. (1985), "The Ritual Experience: Pain and the Transformation of Consciousness in Ordeals of Initiation," *Ethos*, 13(2): 150–174.

Murphy, G. and Medin, D. (1985), "The Role of Theories in Conceptual Coherence," *Psychological Review*, 92: 289–316.

Nagel, E. (1961), *The Structure of Science*, New York: Harcourt, Brace and World.

Nagel, T. (1974), "What Is It Like to Be a Bat?," *Philosophical Review*, 83(4): 435–450.

Neisser, U. (1994), "Multiple Systems: A New Approach to Cognitive Theory," *European Journal of Cognitive Psychology*, 6: 225–241.

Neisser, U., Boodoo, G., Bouchard, T. J., Boykin, A. W., Brody, N., Ceci, S. J., Halpern, D. F., Loehlin, J. C., Perloff, R., Sternberg, R. J., and Urbina, S. (1996), "Intelligence: Knowns and Unknowns," *American Psychologist*, 51: 77–101.

Nielbo, K. L. and Sørensen, J. (2011), "Spontaneous Processing of Functional and Non-functional Action Sequences," *Religion, Brain, & Behavior*, 1(1): 18–30.

Nisbet, R. and Ross, L. (1980), *Human Inference: Strategies and Shortcomings of Social Judgment*, Englewood Cliffs, NJ: Prentice-Hall.

Nisbett, R. and Wilson, T. (1977), "Telling More Than We Can Know: Verbal Reports on Mental Processes," *Psychological Review*, 84: 231–259.

Norenzayan, A. (2013), *Big Gods: How Religion Transformed Cooperation and Conflict*, Princeton, NJ: Princeton University Press.

Norenzayan, A. (2014), "Big Questions about Big Gods: Response and Discussion," *Religion, Brain & Behavior*, 5(4): 266–342.

Norenzayan, A., Atran, S., Faulkner, J., and Schaller, M. (2006), "Memory and Mystery: The Cultural Selection of Minimally Counterintuitive Narratives," *Cognitive Science*, 30(3): 531–553.

Nuckolls, C. (1993), "The Anthropology of Explanation," *Anthropology Quarterly*, 66: 1–22.

Nuckolls, C. (1995). "Motivation and the Will to Power: Ethnopsychology and the Return of Thomas Hobbes," *Philosophy of the Social Sciences*, 25: 345–359.

Obeysekere, G. (1990), *The Work of Culture*, Chicago, IL: University of Chicago Press.

O'Meara, T. (1989), "Anthropology as Empirical Science," *American Anthropologist*, 91: 354–369.

Oppenheim, P. and Putnam, H. (1958), "Unity of Science as a Working Hypothesis," in H. Feigl, M. Scriven, and G. Maxwell (eds), *Minnesota Studies in the Philosophy of Science: Vol. 1*, 405–428, Minneapolis: University of Minnesota Press.

Otto, R. (1958), *The Idea of the Holy*, New York: Oxford University Press.

Pals, D. (1986), "Reductionism and Belief: An Appraisal of the Attacks on the Doctrine of Irreducible Religion," *Journal of Religion*, 66: 18–36.

Pals, D. (1990), "Autonomy, Legitimacy, and the Study of Religion," *Religion*, 20: 1–16.

Penner, H. (1986), "Structure and Religion," *History of Religions*, 25: 236–254.

Penner, H. (1989), *Impasse and Resolution: A Critique of the Study of Religion*, New York: Peter Lang.

Peterson, G. R. (2013), "McCauley, the Maturationally Natural, and the Current Limits of the Cognitive Science of Religion," *Religion, Brain & Behavior*, 3: 141–151.

Popper, K. (1959), *The Logic of Scientific Discovery*, New York: Harper and Row.

Popper, K. (1963), *Conjecture and Refutations*, New York: Harper and Row.

Popper, K. (1972), *Objective Knowledge: An Evolutionary Approach*, Oxford: Oxford University Press.

Preus, J. S. (1987), *Explaining Religion*, New Haven: Yale University Press.

Proudfoot, W. (1985), *Religious Experience*, Berkeley CA: University of California Press.

Putnam, H. (1981), *Reason, Truth and History*, New York: Cambridge University Press.

Pye, M. (1982), "The Study of Religion as an Autonomous Discipline," *Religion*, 12: 67–76.

Pyysiäinen, I. and Uro, R. (eds) (2007), *Explaining Christian Origins and Early Judaism: Contributions from Cognitive and Social Science*, Leiden: Brill.

Rappaport, R. (1979), *Ecology, Meaning, and Religion*, Richmond, CA: North Atlantic Books.

Richerson, P. J. and Boyd, R. (2006), *Not By Genes Alone: How Culture Transformed Human Evolution*, Chicago, IL: University of Chicago Press.

Ricouer, P. (1974), *The Conflict of Interpretation* edited by D. Ihde, Evanston: Northwestern University Press.

Rizzolatti, G., Fadiga, L., Fogassi, L., and Gallese, V. (2011), "From Mirror Neurons to Imitation: Facts and Speculations," in A. N. Meltzoff and W. Prinz (eds), *The Imitative Mind: Development, Evolution, and Brain Bases*, 247–266, Cambridge: Cambridge University Press.

Rorty, R. (1982), *Consequences of Pragmatism*, Minneapolis: University of Minnesota Press.

Rosenberg, A. (1980), *Sociobiology and the Preemption of Social Science*, Baltimore, MD: The Johns Hopkins University Press.

Rosenberg, A. (2006), *Darwinian Reductionism: Or, How to Stop Worrying and Love Molecular Biology*, Chicago, IL: University of Chicago Press.

Rudner, R. (1966), *Philosophy of Social Science*, Englewood Cliffs, NJ: Prentice–Hall.

Saler, B. (1993), *Conceptualizing Religion: Immanent Anthropologists, Transcendent Natives, and Unbound Categories*, New York: Berghahn Books.

Saler, B. (2008), "Conceptualizing Religion: Some Recent Reflections," *Religion*, 38(3): 219–225.

Saler, B. (2009), "Reduction, Integrated Theory, and the Study of Religion," *Religion*, 39: 348–351.

Salmon, W. (1970), *Statistical Explanation and Statistical Relevance*, Pittsburgh, PA: University of Pittsburgh Press.

Savage-Rumbaugh, E. S., McDonald, K., Sevcik, R. Hopkins, W., and Rupert, E. (1986), "Spontaneous Symbol Acquisition and Communicative Use by Pygmy Chimpanzee (*Pan paniscus*)," *Journal of Experimental Psychology: General*, 115: 211–235.

Schjoedt, U., Sørensen, J., Laigaard Nielbo, K., Xygalatas, D., Mitkidis, P., and Bulbulia, J. (2013), "Cognitive Resource Depletion in Religious Interactions," *Religion, Brain & Behavior*, 3(1): 39–55.

Schjoedt, U., Stødkilde-Jørgensen, H., Geertz, A., and Roepstorff, A. (2009), "Highly Religious Participants Recruit Areas of Social Cognition in Personal Prayer," *Social Cognitive and Affective Neuroscience*, 4: 199–207.

Schjoedt, U., Stødkilde-Jørgensen, H., Geertz, A., Lund, T. E., and Roepstorff, A. (2011), "The Power of Charisma—Perceived Charisma Inhibits the Frontal Executive Network of Believers in Intercessory Prayer," *Social, Cognitive, and Affective Neuroscience (SCAN)*, 6(1): 119–127.

Scribner, S. and Cole, M. (1981), *The Psychology of Literacy*, Cambridge: Harvard University Press.

Segal, R. (1989), *Religion and the Social Sciences: Essays on the Confrontation*, Atlanta, GA: Scholars Press.

Shils, E. (1972), *The Constitution of Society*, Chicago, IL: University of Chicago Press.

Shore, B. (1995), *Culture in Mind: Cognitive Dimensions of Cultural Knowledge*, Oxford: Oxford University Press.

Shweder, R. A. (1984), "Anthropology's Romantic Rebellion, or There's More to Thinking than Reason and Evidence," in R. A. Shweder and R. Levine (eds), *Culture Theory: Essays on Mind, Self and Emotions*, 27–66, New York: Cambridge University Press.

Skinner, B. (1953), *Science and Human Behavior*, New York: Macmillan.

Slingerland, E. (2008), *What Science Offers the Humanities: Integrating Body and Culture*, New York: Cambridge University Press.

Slone, D. J. (2004), *Theological Incorrectness: Why Religious People Believe What They Shouldn't*, New York: Oxford University Press.

Slone, D. J., Gonce, L. O., Upal, A., Tweney, R., and Edwards, K. (2007), "Imagery Effects on Recall of Minimally Counterintuitive Concepts," *Journal of Cognition and Culture*, 7: 355–367.

Sosis, R. and Alacorta, C. (2003), "Signaling, Solidarity, and the Sacred: The Evolution of Religious Behavior," *Evolutionary Anthropology*, 12: 264–274.

Sosis, R. and Ruffle, B. J. (2003), "Religious Ritual and Cooperation: Testing for a Relationship on Israeli Religious and Secular Kibbutzin," *Current Anthropology*, 44(5): 713–722.

Spence, D. (1982), *Narrative Truth and Historical Truth*, New York: Norton.

Sperber, D. (1975), *Rethinking Symbolism*, Cambridge: Cambridge University Press.

Sperber, D. (1985), *On Anthropological Knowledge*, Cambridge: Cambridge University Press.

Sperber, D. (1996), *Explaining Culture: A Naturalistic Approach*, Oxford: Blackwell Publishers.

Spiro, M. (1966), "Religion: Problems of Definition and Explanation," in M. Banton (ed.), *Anthropological Approaches to the Study of Religion*, 85–126, London: Tavistock.

Spiro, M. (1987), *Culture and Human Nature*, edited by B. Kilborne and L. L. Langness, Chicago, IL: University of Chicago Press.

Stark, R. and Bainbridge, W. S. (1996), *A Theory of Religion*, New Brunswick, NJ: Rutgers University Press.

Staussberg, M. (ed.) (2014), "Review Symposium on Ara Norenzayan: *Big Gods: How Religion Transformed Cooperation and Conflict*," *Religion*, 44(4): 592–683.

Stich, S. (1983), *From Folk Psychology to Cognitive Science: The Case against Belief*, Cambridge: The MIT Press.

Stich, S. (1990), *The Fragmentation of Reason*, Cambridge: The MIT Press.

Stroop, J. R. (1935), "Studies of Interference in Serial-Verbal Reaction," *Journal of Experimental Psychology*, 18(6): 643–662.

Suppe, F. (1977), *The Structure of Scientific Theories* (2nd ed.), Urbana: University of Illinois Press.

Taves, A. (2009), *Religious Experience Reconsidered: A Building-Block Approach to the Study of Religion and Other Special Things*, Princeton, NJ: Princeton University Press.

Thagard, P. (1992), *Conceptual Revolutions*, Princeton, NJ: Princeton University Press.

Thagard, P. (1999), *How Scientists Explain Disease*, Princeton, NJ: Princeton University Press.

Thagard, P. (2006), *Hot Thought: Mechanisms and Applications of Emotional Cognition*, Cambridge: The MIT Press.

Tillich, P. (1963), *Christianity and the Encounter of World Religions*, New York: Columbia University Press.

Tite, P. (2004), "Naming or Defining? On the Necessity of Reduction in Religious Studies," *Culture and Religion*, 5: 339–365.

Tolman, E. (1967), *Purposive Behavior in Animals and Men*, New York: Irvington.

Tomasello, M., Kruger, A., and Ratner, H. H. (1993), "Cultural Learning," *Behavioral and Brain Sciences*, 16: 495–552.

Tooby, J. and Cosmides, L. (1989), "Evolutionary Psychology and the Generation of Culture: Part 1," *Ethnology and Sociobiology*, 10: 29–49.

Quine, W. V. O. (1953), "Two Dogmas of Empiricism," in *From a Logical Point of View*, 20–46, New York: Harper and Row.

Ungerleider, L. G. and Mishkin, M. (1982), "Two Cortical Visual Systems," in D. J. Ingle, M. A. Godale, and J. W. Mansfield (eds), *Analysis of Visual Behavior*, 549–586, Cambridge: The MIT Press.

Upal, A., Gonce, L. O., Slone, D. J., and Tweney, R. (2007), "Contextualizing Counterintuitiveness: How Context Affects Comprehension and Memorability of Counterintuitive Concepts," *Cognitive Science*, 31: 415–439. DOI: 10.1080/15326900701326568.

Van Der Leeuw, G. (1963), *Religion in Essence and Manifestation: A Study in Phenomenology*, translated by J. E. Turner, New York: Harper and Row.

van Essen, D. C. and Gallant, J. L. (1994), "Neural Mechanisms of Form and Motion Processing in the Primate Visual System," *Neuron*, 13: 1–10.

Von Restorff, H. (1933), "Über die Wirkung von Bereichsbildungen im Spurenfeld (The Effects of Field Formation in the Trace Field)," *Psychological Research*, 18(1): 299–342.

Wach, J. (1988a), *Introduction to the History of Religions*, edited by J. Kitagawa and G. Alles, New York: Macmillan.

Wach, J. (1988b), *Essays in the History of Religions*, edited by J. Kitagawa and G. Alles, New York: Macmillan.

Warren, R. (1970), "Perceptual Restoration of Missing Speech Sounds," *Science*, 167(3917): 392–393.

Wason, P. C. (1966), "Reasoning," in B. M. Foss (ed.), *New Horizons in Psychology*, 135–151, Harmondsworth: Penguin.

Wason, P. C. (1968), "Reasoning about a Rule," *Quarterly Journal of Experimental Psychology*, 20(3): 273–281.

Weber, M. (1964), *The Sociology of Religion*, translated by E. Fischoff, Boston, MA: Beacon.

White, G. (1992), "Ethnopsychology," in T. Schwartz, G. White, and C. Lutz (eds), *New Directions in Psychological Anthropology*, 21–46, Cambridge: Cambridge University Press.

White, L. (1949), *The Science of Culture*, New York: Farrar and Strauss.

Whitehouse, H. (1992), "Memorable Religions: Transmission, Codification and Change in Divergent Melanesian Contexts," *Man (N.S.)*, 27: 777–797.

Whitehouse, H. (1995), *Inside the Cult: Religious Innovation and Transmission in Papua New Guinea*, Oxford: Clarendon Press.

Whitehouse, H. (1996), "Rites of Terror: Emotion, metaphor, and memory in Melanesian initiation cults," *Journal of the Royal Anthropological Institute*, 2(4): 703–715.

Whitehouse, H. (2004), *Modes of Religiosity: A Cognitive Theory of Religious Transmission*, Walnut Creek, CA: AltaMira.

Whitehouse, H. and Laidlaw, J. (eds) (2004), *Ritual and Memory: Towards a Comparative Anthropology of Religion*, Walnut Creek, CA: Alta Mira Press.

Whitehouse, H. and Lanman, J. (2014), "The Ties that Bind Us: Ritual, Fusion, and Identification," *Current Anthropology*, 55(6): 674–695.

Whitehouse, H. and Martin, L. (eds) (2004), *Theorizing Religions Past: Archaeology, History, and Cognition*, Walnut Creek, CA: Alta Mira Press.

Whitehouse, H. and McCauley, R. N. (eds) (2005), *Mind and Religion: Psychological and Cognitive Foundations of Religiosity*, Walnut Creek, CA: AltaMira Press.

Wiebe, D. (1984), "The Failure of Nerve in the Study of Religion," *Studies in Religion*, 13: 401–422.

Wiebe, D. (1985), "A Positive Episteme for the Study of Religion," *The Scottish Journal of Religious Studies*, 6: 78–95.

Wiebe, D. (1988), "Why the Academic Study of Religion?" *Religious Studies*, 24: 403–413.

Willard, A. K., Henrich, J., and Norenzayan, A. (n.d.), The Role of Memory, Belief, and Familiarity in the Transmission of Counterintuitive Content.

Wilson, B. (1970), *Rationality*, New York: Harper and Row.

Wilson, E. O. (1975), *Sociobiology*, Cambridge: Harvard University Press.

Wimsatt, W. (1972), "Teleology and the Logical Structure of Function Statements," *Studies in the History and Philosophy of Science*, 3: 1–80.

Wimsatt, W. (1976), "Reductionism, Levels of Organization, and the Mind-body Problem," in G. Globus, G. Maxwell, and I. Savodnik (eds), *Consciousness and the Brain*, 205–267, New York: Plenum Press.

Wimsatt, W. (1978), "Reduction and Reductionism," in P. Asquith and H. Kyburg (eds), *Current Problems in Philosophy of Science*, 1–26, East Lansing: Philosophy of Science Association.

Wimsatt, W. (1986), "Forms of Aggregativity," in M. Wedin (ed.), *Human Nature and Natural Knowledge*, 259–293, Dordrecht: Reidel.

Wimsatt, W. (1997), "Aggregativity: Reductive Heuristics for Finding Emergence," *Philosophy of Science*, 64: S372–S384.

Wimsatt, W. (2007), *Re-engineering Philosophy for Limited Beings: Piecewise Approximations of Reality*, Cambridge: Harvard University Press.

Winch, P. (1958), *The Idea of a Social Science*, London: Routledge and Kegan Paul.

Xygalatas, D., Konvalinka, I., Roepstorff, A., and Bulbulia, J. (2011), "Quantifying Collective Effervescence: Heart-rate Dynamics at a Fire Walking Ritual," *Communicative and Integrative Biology*, 4(6): 735–738.

Xygalatas, D., Mitkidis, P., Fischer, R., Reddish, P., Skewes, J., Geertz, A. W., Roepstorff, A., and Bulbulia, J. (2013a), "Extreme Rituals Promote Prosociality," *Psychological Science*, 24: 1602–1605.

Xygalatas, D., Schjoedt, U., Bulbulia, J., Konvalinka, I., Jegindø, E., Reddish, P., Geertz, A. W., and Roepstorff, A. (2013b), "Autobiographical Memory in a Fire-Walking Ritual," *Journal of Cognition and Culture*, 13(1–2): 1–16.

Index